THE LAST RIDE IN TO READVILLE

MICHAEL BOUDREAU

ISBN: 978-1-4834-9888-1 (sc)
ISBN: 978-1-4834-9887-4 (e)

Library of Congress Control Number: 2019903023

Lulu Publishing Services rev. date: 03/16/2019

To my beloved brothers and sisters …
This is for you.

PREFACE

Backward, turn backward, O Time, in your flight,
Make me a child again just for tonight!
Mother, come back from that echoless shore,
Take me again to your heart as of yore;
Kiss from my forehead the furrows of care,
Smooth the few silver threads out of my hair;
Over my slumbers your loving watch keep;
Rock me to sleep, mother, rock me to sleep.

—ELIZABETH AKERS ALLEN

So why did I write this book? I suppose authors get this question a lot. Perhaps it is posed more to people like me who, for reasons others don't understand, put fingers to keyboard apparently out of a deeply internal and personal need to achieve catharsis by offering strangers a painful peek into their private life—and by extension, that of an entire family.

Truthfully, the idea for this book began when I was touched by a flood of memory one late fall afternoon. I had stopped for a cup of coffee up on Mission Hill, Roxbury, Massachusetts, a stone's throw from the now-long-gone projects where I had spent a brief but impactful time growing up. I was so touched that I had to write the poem that follows both the preface and the epilogue.

I've been asked to explain what it is that gives me the right to share so openly about anyone else in my family, particularly my parents, and not confine or limit the story to my own experience. Am I exposing private memories in some attempt to heal an anguished inner child or gain some sort of vengeance at their expense?

Well, first, I'd say that this book wasn't written for complete strangers at all. Thinking that it is implies it's a story about a one-of-a-kind, troubled, nomadic family whose history is so unique that to share it with anyone outside the walls of the innumerable roach-infested tenements, apartments, and houses in and around Boston where it took place would mean exposing readers to a tale of unspeakable realities to which they could never relate, not only shocking them but also making us appear freakish. It casts those readers as uncomfortable gawkers—left speechless, perhaps, by the knowledge that such awfulness could exist.

Yet many prospective readers are not strangers at all to stories like this. Many, maybe, came from large families like mine where children struggled with their arbitrary place in the birth order and had to figure out how to grow up and survive an upbringing they suspected from an early age was different from most others. Maybe some had it worse, with no place to hide in the brood or others to lean on to deflect the worst of it.

We are not strangers at all, those of us who share this kinship. We know all too well the realities described in this book. We are not strangers to each other's hearts and minds through our shared experience of being raised by ill-equipped parents who created for us an unpredictable world marked by uncertainty in all things. We are not strangers in the searing memories of our painful physical experiences, including unearned and unpredictable beatings with a belt or the nursing of a tooth so abscessed you had to press your cheek to a freezing windowpane in a long-forgotten bedroom in the projects, trying to do anything you could to ease the pain.

As far as sticking to my own experience, well, isn't my family precisely that? We all may be born into this world as what psychologists call a *tabula rasa* or blank slate, but from the start, it is our parents and family that begin to imprint upon us the perceptions that go on to shape our emotional disposition and attitudes, determining the type of "locus of control" we adopt and orient ourselves with. Do we make things happen on our own, through our own confidence, our own will? Or do things just happen *to* us, beyond our control? Are we going to go through life with a sense of internal self-destiny, or are we restricted to being merely products of all that is external to ourselves and what serendipity brings across our helpless paths? How or why is it that so many from the same family can turn out so very different in spite of sharing the same DNA and growing-up experiences? This book is a lot about all of that.

This book is not a panacea or device intended to reach back in time to heal wounds inflicted so long ago on a man some might suppose is still nurturing them. Nor is it intended to have some sort of cathartic effect—perhaps like the one achieved by Matt Damon in that moment in the movie *Good Will Hunting* when the psychiatrist portrayed by Robin Williams tells Will what he needed to hear all along, snapping the childhood chains that were holding him hostage by telling him, "It's not your fault."

I've known that about myself forever, and I'm all good with that. This book is not about finding fault and placing blame anyway. Rather, it is a lot about forgiving, although maybe not forgetting. It's about learning that the way to break the spell of anyone or any past event that may still have a crippling hold on you is to just let go. Trite but true. Let go of things like seething resentment, as that is a type of sturdy padlock on the emotional chain that binds you to the very thing or person from which you need to free yourself. Letting go happens through true forgiveness; that is the key that will loosen the chain.

I will confess that I have a couple of selfish motives in writing this book, in terms of coming to some sort of closure on the past. The first relates to my recollection of all those years growing up with constant moves and ever-changing addresses and schools; it's sort of like an old slide show that should be sequential but, in my mind, remained out of order. It's as if I was looking through a blurry lens to take a clear picture. In its way, this book helped put some order to my memories and wipe that foggy lens. I must also say that the events in this book are described to the best of my recollection, and I often found the need to shuffle them around for true chronology and geographical accuracy during the writing.

Secondly, I'd hoped to use this book to make a couple of humble requests to any who care to read it—family, friends, and strangers alike. Please offer your prayers for all parents, living or dead, who did not or may not be raising their children the way that they should. This might even include you. Please offer extra special prayers for their children—or on your own behalf, for the grace needed to find the forgiveness for your parents, especially those who've passed away to a higher and harsher judgment. Forgive them enough to pray for them, no matter the past, as so many of them lay elsewhere, mute and in desperate need of God's mercy and beyond any ability to pray for themselves.

I think that's wise, because our own judgment, when it comes, will take into account how well we forgave others. We very well might find ourselves trying, but unable, to cry out for forgiveness of our own. We may then see that the forgiveness we need only comes by way of others' mercy.

HARD TO SAY WHY ON MISSION HILL
PART I

I can never explain it any better than to say they rushed over me once again
As I poured myself out, along with the light, from the warmth of the coffee shop into the night,
Unexpected, like always, yes, those certain sad but somehow hoped-for feelings
That come with some familiar flash of "ah yes" that helps to remind me why they came.

Maybe this time it was my cheeks, which turned now cold and tight, that brought
Me back to 1967, where I ran, lightheaded, under a late November sky
With fingers crossed and frozen, numb, in a pair of wet and crusted snowy brown mittens
That rubbed the tip of my runny nose red and raw as I hurried home thinking up lies.

Or maybe it was because my eyes, squinting at the dimming daylight nuzzling up
Against the soft blue glowing from the edge of the buzzing neon cup
Were now gazing out of my window in the projects at a brilliant but long-lost moon
As it shot scattered beams across those distant treetops that were level with my room.

This time, the tune my mind minstrels had decided to play struck just the particular chords meant
To send me rushing home, back when my head was full and fearful, to a dirty kitchen in Roxbury
Where I saw myself eating, nose filled with the stench of scorched slabs of curled Spam,
With a blank stare as a cockroach walked across my plate, as if in no hurry, as I ate.

Heading to my car, I gulped walnuts of early winter's icy air and blinked with watery eyes,
And wondered yet again how certain chilly windy dusks on a Boston day can so flood my senses
And push deep into my heart those echoing achy pangs that make me ten again.

CHAPTER 1

Reaching into the freezer case jammed full of microwave meals, I could hear her voice croaking in my head from the night before as we discussed the shopping list over the phone: "Get those frozen meat dinners I like—you know, the ones with the corn and mashed potatoes on the side!" Lord forbid I screwed it up and got the one with the mac and cheese and green beans. That would transform otherwise perfectly good food into, in her words, "gahbage." Her Boston accent was still strong, although mine had softened from being away for so many years.

"And oh," she'd said, "get me the medium-sized instead of the *lahdge* diapers this time. They need to fit under my pajamas."

As I'd expected, the Hanscom Air Force Base commissary was crowded. I maneuvered past an old woman who was blocking the aisle with her cart. She was staring and looking confused—or maybe even with longing—at the ice cream case. It was a payday weekend, so the place was full of older retirees wearing their trademark colorful baseball caps with embroidered letters that read *USMC* or *USAF Vietnam Veteran* or made reference to some other branch of military service. Either they or their wives or widows filled the place the first weekend of each month to spend their pension checks on the much-lower-priced groceries and household supplies. The meats and paper products were especially cheap compared to the off-base supermarkets.

I stopped the groaning cart in front of the rows of refrigerated shelves lined with every manner of milk and fruit juice. "This is bloody ridiculous!" I murmured as I put the sixth half-gallon of pulp-free orange juice fortified with calcium into the shopping cart, piling them on top of the dozen frozen Salisbury steak dinners I'd already loaded up, wedging them up against the twenty-pack of adult incontinence pull-ups.

I'd asked her one day, "Why in the world do you have me buy all of these Salisbury steak frozen dinners for you anyway when all you do is rinse the meat under the faucet after you nuke them?"

"I love the meat, but I hate the gravy! It binds me up so bad, so I wash it off. That reminds me: don't forget the graham crackers to help my doo like you did last time! I like the ones in the red box." Yes, she still said childish things like *doo* or *cuckies* when referring to her bathroom habits.

Pushing the overloaded shopping cart up the aisle, I turned to my wife, Jody, and said, "Again, I ask you, how can one person drink three gallons of orange juice in less than two weeks? Freaking crazy!"

"Well, after all, she is struggling to manage her fake diabetes," Jody replied, smirking.

I could see she was enjoying, as she always did, the beginning of my predictable but temporary tantrum at performing my biweekly duty. It seemed to gather momentum in direct proportion to the rate I filled the shopping cart. It's fairer for me to say it was *our* biweekly duty, although I was the one who always plunged into immaturity over it.

Here I was, fifty-five years old. I had been away, serving in the air force both in the states and abroad, for the better part of my adult life. But still, I felt something like that tantrum coming on whenever I was pulled back into what I referred to as dysfunction junction. I'd been free for so long from the trappings of being a day-to-day part of my family—one of the kookiest collections of blood relations anyone could have on the planet. I'd had my military career and made hundreds of friends around the world. I had a wonderful wife and a beautiful home. I even had a master's degree in psychology. I liked to think that I'd moved on. Yet in spite of all that time and space away and having spent a life as different as it could ever be from where I started, my emotions flooded in a swift regression. My mind said *screw you* to any attempt I might make to escape my family's calamity in spite of my worldly experiences and supposed intellect.

It wasn't so much that Jody and I were giving up just about every other Saturday to schlep a shopping cart full of 2 percent milk, pulp-free orange juice, chicken noodle soup, marshmallow cookies, cocoa, Jell-O cups ("Make sure they're sugar-free!"), bologna, Cheerios, adult diapers, Preparation H, etc. to a housebound eighty-one-year-old woman. It was just that I hated the way it took me right back to a time and crazy place from which I had been running all my adult life. These shopping trips made it seem as if I'd never gone away at all. In this place, I learned firsthand about the fight-or-flight response long before any textbook described it to me. I had a clear reminder of why I chose actual flight in 1975. But beyond all that, the automatic edginess I felt was mostly driven by thoughts about whom I was schlepping these groceries to—my mother.

Ah, the joy.

These dreaded trips from the safety of the suburbs into Readville and her depressing world never failed to get my stomach churning. More and more, dealing with her and the constant regurgitation of familial bitterness that came along with those visits only dredged up decades' worth of best-forgotten memories. Why can't people just let crap go?

Jody and I meandered up to the end of the cooler cases, and I grabbed a box of buttermilk waffles and tossed it onto the pyramid of groceries. "That's the list," I said, and we headed to the long checkout line, where most of the elderly patrons were leaning on their carts and sorting through coupons as they shuffled ever closer to the constantly beeping registers.

"I'll drive," Jody said as I slammed shut the trunk, now stuffed with my mother's bounty. We left the base and headed down Route 2A, where we picked up Route 128/95 South and she pointed her BMW toward Dedham and Readville just beyond.

Since I was a military retiree and had access, we always tried to shop for the cheaper groceries at the air force base. My mother was entitled to commissary privileges, just as I was. She earned those when she married a 100 percent disabled veteran some fifteen years after my father, George, had died. Her second husband's name was Henry T. Foley. He was on duty one day in the late 1950s with the Third Platoon, Reconnaissance Company, 656th Tank Destroyer Battalion, and on patrol just north of Seoul when his Jeep hit a huge rut and rolled over into a ditch, ruining his back for life. I was still on active duty and stationed in San Antonio when I learned she'd met Henry. I, like everyone else, was shocked that a sixty-five-year-old who was always miserable by all accounts would appeal to anyone as a potential partner. But Henry was looking at her through a different lens, I suppose.

It was Veteran's Day, and he was selling those little red paper poppies

3

alongside another Korean War veteran at a long folding table outside the exit to the Stop and Shop on Hyde Park Avenue when the magic happened. He was seventy-two and very much still the witty Irishman with a slight brogue that he'd come by somewhat naturally. Although he'd grown up in Dorchester, it was among his clannish relatives who'd come over from Ireland the generation before. He always said the accent was useful for charming the ladies.

It was warm for November, but he was still wearing his signature red plaid flannel shirt, penny loafers with white socks, and a black scully cap with a bright green shamrock pin stuck just off-center at the brim. As Ma walked by the table, he gave her a broad smile before offering his pitch.

"Would ya like to help out your country's veterans today, love?"

At once, Ma began to preen at the attention. She tugged self-consciously at the side edges of her dirty blond wig, snugging it down, and then adjusted her oversized sunglasses with her palms. She took care to keep the menthol cigarette perched between the stained middle and forefingers of her left hand safely pointed away from her synthetic and flammable hair.

"My husband was in the service, and my son is in the air force, so I always buy my poppy!" said Ma, lying in her sexiest voice as she handed Henry a couple of dollars.

"Let me pin that to your lovely sweater, then," said Henry, rising and coming around the table to do the honors.

Smiling with her yellowed dentures, she leaned in a little bit extra to be sure she gave him the best opportunity to make contact with her chest as he pushed the green wire stem through a buttonhole on her lavender sweater and secured it with pride.

"There you go, my love!"

They got to talking and then flirting, and she made sure Henry learned in a hurry that she was a widow. He offered that he was divorced and lived alone too, and then he asked if she liked Irish music, maybe a little dancing, and perhaps a fish-and-chip for lunch the next day at the Carrib Pub just up the road on Center Street. He proposed that would be a nice way to get to know each other a bit. That pub had the freshest scrod and the best pour of Guinness outside of Dublin.

The fish-and-chip lunch turned into walks on Wollaston Beach in Quincy where Ma lived, trips to Fenway Park to catch the Red Sox, and Sunday pot roasts or New England boiled dinner at Ma's place. As normal as those things might sound to the average person, for Ma to be doing them was almost unthinkable to us. She had an apartment on the first floor of an elderly housing complex where she was designated "floor sheriff" or some such lofty title. She took great pains to tell everyone how earnestly she performed her duties, checking in every day on the oldest residents on her floor to make sure they weren't dead or at the very least hadn't fallen down and been lying helpless and out of reach of their emergency cords.

Henry did the cooking, as my mother only knew two cooking methods: boiling and microwaving. All of the normal activities she was now involved in were truly unimaginable to me and my seven siblings. Ma the neurotic, dating? Her agoraphobia and other miscellaneous anxieties were in some sort of remission? That idea was almost as absurd as saying she had been a good mother.

Where had she found this new level of social functioning? we all wondered. Was this some sort of intervention from on high or maybe a demonic possession? Perhaps she was just being that same attention-seeking and horny old lady we knew so well (as we suspected was probably the case). When Henry died ten-plus years after their marriage, as far as I knew and from what I saw, she didn't even cry. I guess it was no surprise that she didn't attend his wake or funeral. She took great pains for years afterward to tell everyone and anyone in a hushed but bitter whisper that they'd never consummated their marriage. Chalk one up for Henry.

As usual, Jody and I were quiet on our ritualistic ride in to Readville, each of us mentally preparing for the gloomy visit to the "loony bin," as we called Gert's place. It was all Jody could do to resist bringing up to me all of the things that were wrong with my mother and the rest of my family and telling me what I *really* should do about it. I knew she was puzzled by my hypersensitivity when pressed to discuss potential courses of action to address the dysfunctional dynamics that surrounded my family. This lifelong dysfunction had led to my mother's essential estrangement from all but three of her eight children, diluting the pool of possible support that could have helped manage her. Now I now found myself the de facto ringmaster in the gloomy circus that had become her life.

"You *really* need to start checking out assisted living for her, Mike. You know that, don't you?" Jody said for the countless time.

"*Yes,* I know, I know. I will!" I said, thinking *here we go again.*

5

"And what's wrong with your sister? She lives two miles away, and here we are, yet again, coughing up another Saturday and a tank of gas. For what? All for some ungrateful old lady who doesn't give a damn about anyone but herself?"

I knew Jody didn't get how I could truly have any sense of obligation. Hell, I couldn't completely explain it myself. I started to tell her why it was really somewhat my father's fault that I dragged her on these trips into Readville every couple of weeks, but finally I just sat there glum, glancing out of the passenger-side window as we sped by the old Polaroid factory on Route 128, nearing Waltham. It wasn't easy being "Mighty Mike," but for whatever reason, I soldiered on.

"Look, it is what it is, okay?" I said, breaking the silence. "Ma burned her bridge with Judy years ago, and even if my sister rebuilt it, the old biddy wouldn't know how or even want to cross it, okay? Let's just let it go, all right?"

"You're right. I'm sorry. I just get so frustrated with …"

"I know, I know—*your* family."

"Sorry. I won't bring it up again!" Jody said.

"Yes you will," I smiled.

"You're right!" she said, both of us laughing at the way we repeated our own silly and predictable dialogue every other Saturday.

I struggled inside—more than even Jody knew—with my powerlessness to change my mother and the past. What could it possibly take to make all of the maddening neuroses, bitterness, resentment, estrangements, and other crap stuffed under the big top of my family's circus magically harmonious? Why did I even try? I felt just as a friend did who once described how trying to fix her family was like moving furniture around the deck of the Titanic.

Why *did* I feel compelled to fix things, especially when the people needing the fixing weren't all that interested in trying to do it themselves? In the military, things were so much easier. You set a shared objective, developed a strategy, and executed an action plan to get things changed. Try as I might, I just couldn't muster a master plan to fix the lifelong conflicts and distress in my family. But I couldn't allow myself to just walk away either.

"Look," I said. "Like we always say, and the docs agree, for our own sanity we have to think of her as mentally ill, that's all, and what matters most is not how horrific she acts, or how bad she tries to make us or anyone feel, but how we control our reactions to her. Not to let her craziness to get into our heads and our lives."

"That's right, that's right, we can't do that," she said, nodding her head in agreement, both of us knowing we'd already allowed those things to happen, and all too often. "Seems like the only time we get tense with each other is …"

"I know, when it comes to my family," I said, finishing her sentence with a sigh.

Jody pulled onto the exit ramp at Route 1 in Dedham, and we took the back road that wrapped around Legacy Place and down past the luxury condos where the Hersey Meter factory, where Dad had worked some thirty-plus years ago, once stood. The condos now shared the property with some newly constructed senior housing. Then it was through Oakdale Square and down the steep hill through the four corners intersection where we crossed over the Boston-Dedham line and into Readville to complete our mission.

Readville is part of the Hyde Park neighborhood of Boston where I graduated high school and made a few million memories playing hockey on the frozen reedy ponds near the Fairview Cemetery. It was called Dedham Low Plains from 1655 until it was renamed in 1847 after a Mr. James Read, a resident and cotton-mill owner, and it was part of Dedham until 1867. It's bordered by the towns of Milton to the south and Dedham to the west. Not many people knew it, but it was home to Camp Meigs during the American Civil War, a training camp for Union soldiers, including those of the famous 54th Massachusetts Infantry portrayed in the film *Glory*.

In the early part of the twentieth century, a pretty well-known harness racing facility called Readville Trotting Park was located there too. That property later became a huge Stop and Shop warehouse and distribution center where we played street hockey in the parking lot, running back and forth chasing an orange plastic ball for hours on Sunday mornings. Now it's just a big warehouse property.

Jody took the right turn off of River Street onto Ernest Avenue, then the first left onto bumpy Sanford Street, and we were there. Jody put the car in park, cut the engine, and popped the trunk from the inside so we could begin trudging up the walk with the groceries. As I lifted myself out of the bucket seat with yet another sigh, I glanced at the living room window of Ma's blue split-level ranch house and could just make out what appeared to be the silhouette of Gollum from the *Lord of the Rings* movie peeking out at us as my mother stood stooped, just out of full sight, in the shadow of the sheer drape that had been pulled aside by the bony fingers of her gnarled hand.

CHAPTER 2

My childhood is streets upon streets upon
streets upon streets. Streets to define
you and streets to confine you, with no
sign of motorway, freeway or highway.

—MORRISSEY

---

anford Street sat just one block in from River Street, which ran east from the Dedham town line all the way through Cleary Square in Hyde Park before continuing over to Mattapan Square and ending all the way over in Dorchester. From Ma's living room window, you could see Boston Mayor Eddie Menino's smallish ranch-style house with its old-fashioned awnings over the windows facing the street, as it sat almost kitty-corner from hers. It was his childhood home, and he still spent some of his time there, so the Boston police cruiser that provided a security detail was parked by the curb in its usual spot.

It was common practice for the mayor to issue a high volume of reverse-911 calls to Boston residents letting them know about things like a change to the garbage pickup day or reminding the elderly to lock their doors at all times with the growing crime rate. Ma would actually think it was the mayor calling her personally. She took great pride in their relationship.

I knew Sanford Street well—as it seemed I did most of the streets across the entire city of Boston. Our family had done a couple of tours in Readville and Hyde Park over the years, so I was particularly familiar with this neighborhood. Back in the early seventies, we lived just about a mile down the street in what was then a brand-new duplex in Edson Terrace.

It was a small cul-de-sac, and my friends and I would spend hours playing street hockey after dark under the sole street lamp until neighbors starting yelling at us to stop making such a racket. There was a lady who lived across the court from us who was so heavy we could hear the bottom of her rusted out El Dorado squeal as the convertible scraped the ramp of her driveway, the screeching sound indicating to all within earshot that she'd returned home.

Ma had lived in the house on Sanford Street for almost ten years now after moving there with Henry from their first home in Braintree. When Henry died, he'd left her the house along with his veteran's pension. Her time living on Sanford Street was a record for her—maybe for any Boudreau, including myself, even though I had lived in the same place in San Antonio for almost five years, and of course over ten years now in my home in Tyngsboro since Jody and I got married. Once Ma married Georgie and the kids started coming, she became an instrumental part of the constant cycle of packing and repacking as they moved us around like a wandering tribe.

I was born in 1956, and by the time I reached my eighteenth birthday and enlisted in the air force, we'd easily moved more than seventy-five times. For most people, the idea of moving around like that might seem a bit strange. But my family wasn't most people. What would have been *most* strange to my seven brothers and sisters and I would have been something like actually finishing any one particular grade in any one particular school in any one particular year in or around the city of Boston.

Ours was a nomadic childhood marked by the endless drill of packing and unpacking. These moves were most often done surreptitiously to avoid the unsuspecting about-to-be-abandoned landlord, and they took place like clockwork whenever the rent went into arrears for a month or two and the landlord's demands got urgent. For us kids, these moves were a blur of maladjustments and attempts at readjustments through just about every neighborhood and associated school within the greater Boston radius.

One day in the late sixties, I was playing street hockey in the working-class streets of Roslindale—Poplar Street, I think—dodging cars with my friends. The next week, I was sprinting home from my new school, maybe being chased through the maze of red brick buildings, chain-link fences, and sooty incinerators of the Mission Hill projects in Roxbury. Some months later, I was catching the bus from Forest Hills to our new flat in Cleary Square, and then six months after *that*, I was helping to lug a

U-Haul full of busted-up furniture and plastic trash bags full of clothes with their hitchhiking cockroaches up three flights to our next "new house" in that Readville duplex in Edson Terrace.

Whenever we moved, we'd race through the empty and echoing apartment or house scavenging through the closets, basement, or attic to find any booty that might have been left by the previous occupants. I headed right for the high top shelves of closets, because they often yielded the best treasures, like an old baseball card or a couple of dusty coins. Attic beams were good too. Stuff may have been hidden and forgotten there for decades.

Even much later, in 1976, coming back to Boston on military leave from the air force in the wee hours of a crisp November morning, I was reminded that I could never be sure where "home" would be. I remember smiling as the cabbie dumped me on the sidewalk in front of the triple-decker on Central Street in Hyde Park, not far from the William Barton Rogers Junior High School, at two in the morning into a whipping and freezing wind. Pleased with myself, I walked up the creaky porch steps and approached the first floor apartment. "Mighty Mike" was about to pull off a surprise visit from my base in Brindisi, Italy.

The doorbell was hanging by a wire. Just as I went to rap my knuckles on the door, I glanced to my right into a curtainless and empty living room. The inside of the apartment was barely visible in the light offered by the bright moon, but I could see its emptiness well enough. I guess the surprise was on me. Turned out that in their last letter to me a couple of months before, they'd forgotten to let me know about their latest eviction. That was a word we kids used to hate hearing. We'd whisper it to each other the way we heard adults say *cancer*.

One of those evictions found us moving to Dedham (the only time we had ever lived outside of the city of Boston). We were living high on the hog, with each of us actually getting a portion of a piece of a cube steak and some baked potatoes and canned green beans for dinner. Dad was feeling generous because he'd made a few bucks from hitting his numbers. As the breadwinner, he had such food reserved for him most nights, while we'd eat something like mac 'n' cheese from the box or maybe a bowl of gluey cream of chicken soup stirred into rice.

I never knew how Dad swung that move to Dedham, where we lived in a real house for the very first time, and where there were four bedrooms to accommodate all ten of us in rare comfort. It was a world away from the cramped three-bedroom apartments we were used to, with my brothers and me in one bedroom and all five of my sisters crammed into another. We spent most of our childhood sleeping in dilapidated bunk beds, rickety from so many moves and the constant taking apart and putting together.

We all knew the place in Dedham was way beyond my father's budget, so we figured he must have hit the numbers pretty good to be able to put down a security deposit and first month's rent. We also knew our stay would be short-lived, as it indeed turned out to be. But that was our normal. Meanwhile, we'd enjoy living in such an uppity town, although we were treated at school as if we were the Beverly Hillbillies because of our hard Boston accents, shabby clothes, and rotting teeth.

It was a big brown house one lot in from the Gulf gas station at the corner of Route 1 and Dedham Square, and it sat right across from the Dedham Savings Bank. Just after we moved in, we looked out the front window and saw dozens of people moving about, frantic and shouting and emptying tractor-trailer trucks and setting up enormous lighting systems and big cameras, although it was the middle of a brutally hot and humid day. We sent my sister Diane across the street to check things out, as by now we'd all moved out to the front porch, dying with curiosity. Soon she ran back across the street.

"What's going on over there?" my mother asked.

"It's a movie!" Diane said. "They're making a movie!"

"What?" I said. "What about?"

"Gangsters or something," Diane said. "They're going to rob the bank for the movie!"

I could see movie cameras and other equipment being put together and mounted now as some order seemed to be coming to the chaos across the street. Members of the crew were sitting on the grass and the curb smoking cigarettes and talking with animated hands. I noticed the sign for Dedham Savings Bank had been changed to read *South Shore Savings Bank*. I walked off the porch and, trying to seem casual, sauntered across the street to see what more I could find out.

"Hey," I said to one of the younger crew members who looked about twenty. "What's the movie gonna be?"

"Hey, how ya doin'?" the kid replied. "It's a Mob movie. Called *The Friends of Eddie Coyle*. Robert Mitchum is in it."

I learned later that the movie about Eddie Coyle (a.k.a. Eddie Fingers) was based on a true story about an aging delivery-truck driver for a bakery in the Boston area who was also a low-level gunrunner for a crime organization in Boston. As the story went, he was facing several years in prison for a truck hijacking in New Hampshire set up by a guy named Dillon who owned a local bar. Coyle's last chance was a sentencing recommendation from an Alcohol, Tobacco, and Firearms agent, Dave Foley, that Coyle become an informer. Coyle's undercover work got him involved in bank robberies and other unsavory activities. The bank's name had been changed to match the real-life bank robbed in Braintree or Quincy. Unbeknownst to Coyle, Dillon was an informer for Foley, and Coyle wound up getting double-crossed in the end.

"Wow, no kidding," I said. No sooner had that come out of my mouth than I saw Robert Mitchum, the man himself, standing back and off to the side talking with a man I assumed must be the director or someone else important. He was just fifteen feet away. They were gesturing toward an older model car with some actors with masks on already seated inside, with a white screen set up behind the back window and brilliant camera lights on either side.

"What are they going to do over there?" I asked, pointing to the car.

"Ah, they're setting up the getaway scene," the kid replied. "They don't really drive at all. They just sit in the car and pretend, and in the final movie, it will look like they're driving."

"Huh?" I replied.

"Yeah, they just project a movie onto that screen back there, and it looks like they're driving. All the actor has to do is turn the wheel to make it look real."

"Whaddya know? Thanks," I said and darted back across the street to explain everything.

"Robert Mitchum?" Ma said. She instinctively began to tug at the sides of her wig and adjust her stretchy pants and tube top. "Run in the house and get me my sunglasses," she said to no one in particular. Diane got up and went into house to grab them off the kitchen counter where Ma always left them. She was back in no time. Ma put the sunglasses on, adjusted them under her wig and behind her ears, and lit a cigarette as she stood leaning on the porch rail in what I suppose she thought was a sexy pose.

We watched as Robert Mitchum stood by observing as the actors in the car ran through their scene. Suddenly, they piled out of the hot car after a number of takes to take a break. We looked on in amazement as none other than Robert Mitchum walked toward our porch with some other guy who appeared to be one of the crew. They stopped at the stoop, and as Robert Mitchum pushed his fedora up on his head, revealing a sweaty brow, the other guy asked if they might have some cold water, since it was so damn hot out there.

We all just stared unsure and in disbelief for a second, until my mother snapped us out of it by saying, again to no one in particular, "Go in quick and get some ice water for Mr. Mitchum!"

This time, Diane and I both raced in. As she reached for a couple of plastic Tupperware tumblers, I cracked open an ice tray from the freezer. It was the only thing in there. We rushed to fill the tumblers with ice and cold tap water, and then we brought them out front and handed them to my mother, who handed them to the actor and the other guy. The men drained the plastic cups in unison and in one long drink, and with a satisfied "ah," handed them back to my mother.

"Thanks," said the other guy. Robert Mitchum tipped his hat without a word, and they turned and walked back to the bank. Thus ended the Boudreau family's brush with fame. We didn't even have time to ask for an autograph!

Other than that house in Dedham, we were transient residents of traditional Boston neighborhoods like "Rozzie" or Jamaica Plain, with us kids finding creative ways to make palatable our typical dinner of heavily salted and buttered white rice, a slab of government cheese, and a fried chunk of their version of Spam, labeled "chopped meat" on the can. It wasn't as disgusting as the mystery meat labeled "chipped beef" that also came in tins that were as big as paint cans. It was supposed to be beef, but its burgundy color made it the most suspicious of the larder we knew as "surplus food." Plus, it smelled like dog food. Sometimes Ma would mix it with watered-down tomato sauce to put over spaghetti for supper on Sundays.

Perhaps only the peanut butter was more disgusting. It, too, opened like a paint can, and like paint, we'd have to stir in the inch or so of greasy peanut oil floating on the top into the dark brown muck that lay beneath until it was smooth enough to spread.

It's funny how all the childhood memories from all those individual moves—with their apartments and neighborhoods and schools—each somehow has its own unique, indelible, and vivid images, yet when stitched together across the years of constant roaming, they become more of a fuzzy chronological scramble, like a slideshow that is out of order. Memories of home sweet home for us are more of an enormous collage of packing, unpacking, moving trucks, first-floor flats, third-floor apartments, back-alley fire escapes, angry landlords, corner-store credit never to be paid back, pallets of government surplus food, Dad's mastery at staying one step ahead of the bill collectors, his unpredictable wrath and its consequences, Ma's chronic neuroses and associated "nervous breakdowns," and somehow, all the while, us kids pulling each other along despite a life under the rule of ill-equipped parents, with an endless stream of unpredictable and undeserved beatings and those dreaded but eventual evictions.

"Remember that time Dad had the electric bill put in your name back on Lamartine Street?" my oldest sister, Diane, once chuckled.

"Yeah," I said. "Not bad for a six-year-old, huh? Except it was on Green Street, not Lamartine."

One New Year's Eve, all but a couple of us were having a get-together at my sister Karen's house, feasting on lobster ravioli and enjoying probably too many bottles of good red wine, when we decided to play one of our favorite games: Name That House! The rules were pretty simple. The first was, you had to share a unique first-person recollection from our childhood, not repeat one heard and remembered from a tale already told by any of the others. Next, you had to name the street and the neighborhood where the memory or event occurred (knowing the house number was a bonus). The last rule was that the memory had to be corroborated by at least one other sibling. We'd go around the table laughing in hysterics at some long-forgotten (or *repressed*, as we'd often say) memory that, once resurrected, would resonate with some or all of us. Then we'd do a shot of Jameson's Irish whisky or maybe Sambuca.

It wasn't unusual when we played this game, laughing at the funny and the absurd about our growing up, to get the event right but the place wrong, or vice versa. It was also true that our father often employed the tactic of using our names to obtain credit or to reestablish an account of some sort. Each of the eight of us (five girls, three boys) had, at one time or another, been in arrears to the phone company, the electric company, or some other creditor—most long before the age of twelve. Thanks to Dad, we'd joke, most of our credit ratings were probably already shot before we even got to the sixth grade. With eight kids, each having a first, middle, and confirmation name, the number of combinations from which to choose when he needed to establish a new account was impressive.

"Georgie," as my Nana Boudreau used to call him, was a master at working out a way to beat the system (welfare system, tax system, health system, etc.). His skills as a parent, however, weren't so impressive. This, of course, made him the perfect match for Trudy.

Each of them was void of any real personal capacities to parent. They worked in twisted tandem, but each in his or her own way, to portray the world to us as a constant reflection from one of the mirrors in the psychological fun house they had created for us. It was a place where the overriding and steady message was that life is strictly what happens to you; you certainly don't happen to *it*. They certainly happened to us.

Their constant message, unspoken or otherwise, was that everything about your life was under their unchallenged control, and there was no interest whatsoever regarding how you might feel about pretty much anything. You jumped at any orders given. You moved to wherever their eviction took you. You ate whatever they put in front of you. You endured the aching tooth until it rotted and crumbled. You went to bed at six o'clock in the summertime while your friends were still out playing because "I told you so." Above all, your first duty was to make sure Ma was taken care of.

They kept everything topsy-turvy and unpredictable and *different* from everyone else we knew. Somehow I sensed from when I was very young that if we were ever to come to live as full and "normal" a life as we could, in the end, each of us would have to find our own window looking out from that crazy house to see the real world, not the one they'd created, and we'd better head toward it or be doomed to a future much like the one my parents had and were building for us within those walls. We would have to find a window from which to see as best we could our own path to whatever it was that had to be better out there. But as it would turn out, not everyone ended up with an equal view.

CHAPTER 3

When I was a child looking at my parents'
lives, you know what I thought? I thought
heartbreaking. Now I think heartbreaking,
but also insane. Also very funny.

—LOUISE GLUCK

---

reached into the trunk and grabbed the handles of as many of the plastic grocery bags as I could to begin the shuttle back and forth to the blue split-level ranch. It always took us at least two trips up the crumbling walk to get everything dumped onto the Formica counters in the dated galley kitchen that looked just as it had back in the 1970s. Jody had already carried an impressive first load into the house, so I figured I could manage the rest of it in one more load. I put the bags I'd gathered in my right hand onto the ground and slammed the trunk shut.

I regathered the bag handles and waddled up the walk toward the door, balancing all ten bags like two giant buckets of water. I glanced up and saw that the gutter was hanging loose at one end of the roof line and the fake-icicle Christmas lights my brother-in-law had put up along the same line were still there. It was June.

Jody was in the kitchen wedging frozen TV dinners and waffles into an already overstuffed freezer. Now *she* was the one muttering, and I was smirking as I climbed the dirty rug up the short flight of stairs that faced the kitchen, the acrid smell of cigarette smoke already watering my eyes. The air was hot and oppressive. First thing we always did when we got home from the "loony bin" was strip off our clothes and put on a load of laundry.

"Hi, Ma," I said as I crested the top stair and glanced over to her sitting on my right.

"Hi," she said in a weak voice as she rocked gently to and fro on the edge of her dirty blue electric recliner, her head in her hands. *Yep, another day in her paradise,* I thought, shaking my head. Ma pretty much lived her life sitting in that chair, day in and day out, and for no apparent reason other than to accentuate the appearance of helplessness and suffering. Other than trips to the doctor or the bathroom, she stayed put, as though bedridden. She was spry enough to run with care up and down the hallway or take the short two flights of stairs to the basement when it suited her, but she preferred to appear anchored and unable to move to amplify her appearance of misery.

Plus, she was lazy.

I took the few quick steps into the kitchen and plunked the rest of the groceries onto the small round maplewood kitchen table. It was littered with half-eaten loaves of wheat bread, stale marshmallow cookies, and an assortment of tubes of ointments like KY Jelly and Preparation H. Already annoyed, I reminded myself that I wouldn't be here long and just deal with it.

"I'll put these away. You go ahead and visit," Jody said, sounding just a little too generous.

"Gee thanks," I said, smiling and rolling my eyes.

I stepped back into the living room. Ma had by now completed her infantile rocking and resumed her more typical position: sitting all the way back now in the recliner, legs crossed, smoking a Benson and Hedges Menthol Light 100 that came from the flip-box pack. No soft pack for her. Once I forgot to get them in menthol, and she refused to smoke them. Another time, I forgot the "100," and those too stayed on the dining room table, unsmoked. She eventually gave them to my oldest sister, who was always short of cash. Ma doled them out pack by pack as Diane completed duties and errands—and, of course, performed the requisite amount of groveling.

I took a peek at the cuckoo clock I'd bought for her while stationed in Germany, one of the many clocks in the room. It was about twenty minutes to one. I had skipped breakfast save for a quick glass of milk with my morning medications, and my stomach was growling. We always rewarded ourselves for doing our Readville duty by stopping at our favorite fish restaurant in Chelmsford on the way home. We always sat at the bar, and the bartender, Scott—knowing our every-other-Saturday ritual—would, with genuine sympathy, start to set up our drinks before we even got nestled on our stools. Then he'd smirk at us and say, "Hey kiddies, how's Mom today?"

I bent over and kissed her on the forehead—a light kiss, the only appearance of affection I could muster at all anymore. My ritualistic visits pretty much always started this way. On days we'd come over, she'd keep that furtive watch for when we pulled up to the front of the house, then scurry to the recliner, having already prepared the stage. Lights off? Check. Television off? Check. Sad face? Check. As soon as she heard the key in the lock, she'd either lean back in the chair with her eyes half-closed with a weak expression on her face or forward with her head in her hands and commence her rhythmic rocking.

Knowing all this, we spoke with her psychiatrist about it. He said that it was important that no one "enable this manipulative behavior" by giving it any acknowledgement. At first, it was difficult to ignore, but the doctor was right. If we ignored it, she'd give up the ruse, frustrated by no reaction, and in short order revert to her usual sarcastic martyrdom.

I moved back a couple of steps and perched myself on the overstuffed arm of the couch, just to her left, taking my established position for our short twenty-minute-or-so visit. That was what our relationship, beyond weekly phone calls, had now boiled down to. Jody and I didn't like to sit at all on any of her furniture ever since the bedbug infestation, but I felt safe enough on that small patch of material.

I began with my perfunctory, "So how are you feeling today?"

"Shitty! What do you think?" she said, exhaling another plume of smoke into the always hazy room. Looking over her shoulder, I could see varying streams of caramel-colored nicotine working their way down the wall in the foyer like some sort of alien goo.

"Jeez, Ma, it's always so dark in here," I said as I leaned over and flipped the light switch on the wall next to her curio cabinet, which was within my reach. The cabinet was filled with souvenir bells I had given her from so many of the places I'd traveled around the world. They hadn't been touched in years by the looks of them; they just sat there, dusty and silent. There was the Waterford crystal one I'd sent from a trip to Ireland and next to it a porcelain one with the Pope's smiling image I'd picked up for her in Rome at a shop near the Vatican.

It was a humid day, and the house was buttoned up, as it always was.

Between the thick stench of cigarette smoke and a somewhat moldy odor that permeated the place, it had the institutional smell of a nursing home. In spite of the heat, Ma was dressed in her standard garb: ratty pink terry cloth robe over flannel pajamas with tattered baby blue fur-lined slippers covering her swollen feet. The robe was a Mother's Day present, and although just a month old, it was dotted with cigarette burns.

I hadn't given her a birthday card to go along with the gift, since I'd long since stopped trying to find just the right one with the right kind of words inside. I used to spend an hour at the Hallmark store looking them over, trying to find something generic, but all of them seemed to have sentiments that just weren't consistent with the truth of how I felt about her. They said things like, "A mother's love is unlike any other, and I'm so glad you've given me yours." Or "Thank you, Mother, for always being there, guiding, protecting, loving …" Yuck. Talk about not applicable. Of course, the same problem applied to finding a card that wasn't as nauseating for any other holiday as well, so I just gave it up.

I could see she was neglecting her chin hairs again. She had visits twice a week from the city's senior services to help her with hygiene and to take care of such things. The woman had just been there the day before, but I could see Ma hadn't been helped to thoroughly bathe and groom. Not that this was ever important to her. Her siblings used to call her "Dirty Gerty" when she was growing up because of her unimpressive grooming habits.

I made a mental note to call the agency on Monday, but I was sure they'd tell me they'd tried to do their job but she wouldn't cooperate. With so few family members willing to help, I made sure I researched and acquired any and all available outside assistance I could, since we lived over an hour away. Between the visiting nurses, the housekeeper, and the senior services agency, I felt that at least she was getting the highest level of care she could afford and to which she was entitled.

She looked haggard even beyond her eighty-one years and seemed to like it that way, as it enhanced her victimized appearance, one that she worked very hard to sustain so all the world could see just how sick, neglected, and lonesome she was, abandoned and shunned by most of her children, even after all she'd done for them. That's how she'd put it to anyone who'd listen. Her eyes were red, with puffy bags beneath.

The pale skin on her forearms was specked with random red and scaly blotches, different from the ones she'd had before from the bedbug bites. My sister Loretta had brought those into the house the year before in one of the trash bags of clothing she'd brought in during a brief stay with Ma between group homes. We had to throw practically everything out when getting rid of those creatures and spent two full days at the laundromat in East Dedham after emptying all of the dresser drawers and closets, washing every stitch of clothing in scalding hot water, and drying on the highest heat setting. We must have pumped over a hundred dollars in quarters into the slots of those machines to get the job done—and of course, we had to replace her mattress and box spring.

That bedbug episode was yet another unpleasant reminder of childhood and the years of living with those damn omnipresent cockroaches that stood among nature's hardiest survivors over the millennia. We'd all learned to freeze for a moment when turning on the kitchen light in the morning before the sun came up to give them a moment to scuttle back into the floorboards and cupboards or under the refrigerator to avoid the most unpleasant sensation of stepping on one with a bare foot. They were just a disgusting part of life that I'd put out of my mind. But when I saw those garish welts all over my mother's arms, I investigated her bedroom and, in turning over her mattress, was horrified to see a massive colony of moving brown dots that made my skin crawl as much as the cockroaches had. Although we did the best we could and there'd been no sign they'd returned, I knew they'd be back sometime.

Ma was starting to become more stooped-over these days, her height having slipped all the way down to five feet, one inch, according to her last doctor's visit. Her unnecessary walker was in its perpetual position facing her chair, serving as a one-stop shop for all things dear in her small world. An oversized purse hung from one of the grips, and the basket in front was full of pill bottles, half-consumed liters of diet ginger ale, and adult diapers. She always wore those in case she couldn't make it down the hall, she said, to do her "cuckies."

Her most prized possession, however, was on the walker's seat, within easy reach—her plastic bottle of diabetic test strips. No matter that she wasn't diabetic and didn't need to check her glucose at all. The doctor had mentioned to her some fifteen years back that she had "elevated" blood sugar and that it might be a good idea to check it once in a while as she monitored her diet. There was no way he could have known that his simple instructions would morph into a finger-pricking obsession that now dominated my mother's waking moments.

Her regimen called for her to check her blood sugar twice a day—once in the morning after fasting all night and the other in the middle of the afternoon after eating—so the prescription was doled out by the doctor one hundred strips at a time, intended to last fifty days before refilling. These days, it wasn't uncommon for her to prick her finger at least ten to fifteen times a day, so she was always running short. Panic would set in as her supply dwindled, since she knew that the pharmacy wouldn't refill it earlier than scheduled. She'd scheme a way to convince Diane to buy them over the counter without telling Mighty Mike, offering her gas money or cigarettes as a bribe. Diane would not always keep me in the loop, but I didn't care much at this point.

Ma would even bother the neighbors from time to time if she got desperate enough. That was a daily double for her, as she could then take the opportunity to tell them just how much her children neglected her and how she was so alone and abandoned. Fortunately, they were wise to her, as I'd chat with them from time to time in the driveway. They were well aware of the comings and goings of myself, a couple of my sisters, and all the home-care services. They were all very gracious after I'd apologized to each of them at one time or another, but I still gave them my business card and urged them to give me a call if she became too much of a nuisance.

Ma was on a very fixed income, and I brought her a limited amount of spending money along with the groceries every other week. She hoarded the cash to make sure she could get her "fix" once the prescription of those diabetic test strips started to run out. I couldn't stand to see her waste her money on fulfilling her obsession, but I finally stopped trying to reason with her. I'd had to take away her checkbook months earlier to prevent her from bouncing checks as she had been in an attempt to stockpile the strips. As stupid as it was, she could jab herself like a deranged mosquito a hundred times a day as far as I was concerned as long as she didn't spend more than her allowance. Besides, I knew it made her feel good to be sneaky.

When we were kids, she'd siphon off a dollar here or there or keep the change from any money my father would give her to send us to the corner store, or she'd maybe lift a buck or two now and again right from his wallet or after taking care of a paid bill, which was rare. She had to be extra careful about daring to take from his wallet, though, since Georgie usually didn't have much and she'd likely be caught. It was best that she do that after he came back from a successful visit with the bookie.

She called this money her "sneakies" and kept it in squirreled away in a small red purse with a clasp that made a loud click when she'd shut it. Once in a while, one of us would get a little of her stash as hush money when she didn't want my father to find out about one of her furtive "stops" while running errands. I could sometimes even get her to cough up five bucks for a new hockey stick, but that was rare. Most times, we'd get just enough to go to the corner store and get ourselves a "tonic" and a package of cupcakes for fifty cents that would further escalate the number of cavities in our already rotting teeth.

She was on more than ten medications now, ranging from baby aspirin to a psychotropic that in theory helped her manage her anxiety attacks. Her go-to strategy, really her only strategy throughout her life, was to become "anxious" when faced with any situation that displeased her or to explain away what to all of us kids was her inexplicable and mind-numbing helplessness or her apathy when it came to our nurturing, well-being, and chiefly our vulnerability to Georgie's threats and terror tactics.

Save for the clozapine, which was to be taken four times a day, all of the other medications were to be ingested once daily—say all at once in the morning. Easy. But oh no, not for Trudy, who turned what should have been a simple regimen into a complex scheduling system that featured spacing out each of the medicines in bizarre intervals and tracking, to the minute, the time between each gulp of orange juice she'd use to wash the medication down in exaggerated fashion. She kept dozens of clocks all over the house, any of which would bong or clang at the top or bottom of every hour signaling her that it was time. If she happened to be on the toilet and heard one of them go off, she'd clamor to her feet, pull up her diaper, and race to her pill cases and bottle of orange juice.

After swallowing the pill with an audible gulp, she'd dutifully write down the date and time in her chicken scratch into one of dozens of small colorful spiral notebooks that littered the end table and the coffee table and were strewn on the floor all around her chair. There must have been at least five years' worth of her useless scribbling. It was the same with the incessant and needless checking of her blood glucose levels. Each result was catalogued by date and time.

Whenever anyone took her to her monthly doctor's appointment, she'd be sure to bring along a couple of her latest log books to show the doctor, with the pride of a three-year-old who'd drawn a picture all by herself. He'd always say to her without looking up as he made his notes, "That's wonderful, Gertrude. My, aren't you organized!"

Each visit to her house, she'd give me her pill schedule rundown for what would seem like the millionth time.

"Ma," I'd say. "I get it. I know *all* of your pills and when you take them. You don't need to explain it to me every time you see me."

"I'm sorry," she'd whimper. "I just wanted you to know how good I'm doing."

As always, her dirty blond wig sat to her right, pulled a bit askew down onto a foam mannequin head. Both wig and head were well over forty years old. They sat on an old end table that separated her chair from the battered Queen Anne chair where Henry always used to sit reading his paper and eating jelly beans in his pajamas. His tattered leather slippers were still under the dilapidated footstool, right where he'd left them before he died.

Her natural hair had always been thin and wispy, and now it was barely even thick enough to brush. I'm not sure when she started wearing the wig whenever she left the house, but she also wouldn't be caught dead without it if company dropped by or any of us brought a friend home without warning, which was rare. If caught by surprise, she'd shriek and run down the hall shouting, "Don't bring them in until I put on my head!"

She'd been a huge country music fan when she was younger, and she'd sing along to Patsy Cline or Tammy Wynette as we listened to the AM radio when she'd drive us around on errands in the old Plymouth station wagon with the wood side panels and rotting floorboards. Her favorite song was Tammy's "D-I-V-O-R-C-E," or maybe Eddie Arnold's "Please Release Me." She seemed to favor songs that spoke of someone trapped in a relationship with the wrong person and from which there was no way out, contributing to our belief that my father was someone from whom she should be rescued and whom we should also fear.

On rare occasions, we'd go to places like Bradlees or Zayre department stores, both long out of business now, for the cheapest back-to-school or Easter clothes if we were getting any that year, but most times we'd go to visit relatives like Nana Bovaird, Aunty Kay, or some others on Calumet Street high up on Mission Hill, with Ma's wig always secure and in place. I always thought maybe she wore the wig, along with those omnipresent giant sunglasses, because we all knew she fancied herself a country music sexpot of some sort, and she thought it helped her resemble her idol, Ms. Wynette.

No matter where we went, she was always flirting with other men. In one case, it took us a while to figure out why she made so many stops at this one Sunoco gas station on Hyde Park Avenue, even when she didn't need any gas, to talk to this Italian guy with an embroidered patch that said "Joe" sewn above the left pocket of his dark blue gas-station-attendant shirt. He'd lean in her window smiling, and the two of them would blow cigarette smoke at each other from the corners of their mouths, talking and laughing in soft tones as we sat in the back seat bored.

Sometimes Joe would toss us a package of M&Ms or some other candy, so we didn't always mind. She made plenty of such stops elsewhere over the years. There was also a guy who'd stop by sometimes after Dad had gone to work and we'd not yet left for school who also worked at an Esso gas station, this one in Dedham. His name, "Phil," was also embroidered over the pocket of his work shirt. He'd knock on the door, and one of us would let him in. Ma would yell from her bedroom to let him come on down, where she'd be lying on the bed in her pajamas and robe. Ma would yell for one of us to make Phil a "cup of Sanka," and he would sit at the edge of her bed as they talked in whispers until we'd all left the house. She'd explained to us when Phil first started coming around that he was a "special friend," which everyone needed. I supposed gas-station attendants made the best listeners?

We all knew Phil from that Esso station on the Dedham-Readville line that my father always stopped into. We'd be stuck in the back seat there as well as they yukked it up together and sometimes traded porn magazines. We weren't sure if my father knew about Phil's morning stops to our apartment for coffee with Ma, but he knew of Ma and Joe being chummy, because one Saturday afternoon Joe came to visit us when we lived on Walworth Street in Roslindale, and the three of them locked themselves in the living room, barricading the door with the long stereo cabinet and turning it up loud after telling all of us to go outside and play.

Playing detective, Karen and I snuck back into the house and put our ears to the door. All we could hear was very loud Frank Sinatra songs over occasional laughter and muffled voices. We could only wonder what the hell they were doing.

We'd moved to Walworth Street from that roach-infested apartment in the Mission Hill projects, and in that move, it was as though we'd found sanctuary from the constant threat of an environment that required us kids to keep constant watch over our shoulders and some days literally run from building to building to ensure safety. Nonetheless, I always associated our stint on Walworth Street with locked doors, whispers, and family secrets—and not just because Joe wasn't the only man to visit my mother and father behind a shut door. It was while living there that my mother gave birth to my youngest sister, Susan, and as was typical, all of us kids got farmed out to stay with relatives for a few days while she was in the hospital. That is, all of us except for Diane this time—as we were told she'd be staying home alone with our father.

I didn't think much of it as I grabbed my brown grocery bag stuffed with a few days' change of clothes and headed to the car where Dad and the others were waiting so he could shuttle us to various relatives' houses, all either in Jamaica Plain or Roxbury, to be dropped off and wait for the news of our newest brother or sister and when we'd get to come home. It was April, and we were pulled out of school as we always were if school was in session when Ma was having another one of us. I couldn't wait, as I knew Nana would always make something special for dinner like spaghetti and meatballs for the first night of my stay over.

I was there only two nights when my grandmother told me that I had a new baby sister and my father would be by to pick me up later in the afternoon on what was the third day of my visit. It had been a fun two days skipping school and running the streets and exploring the rocky outcropping on Mission Hill that overlooked Brigham Circle with some of my cousins and their friends who lived close by. But I was looking forward to getting home to my baseball glove and a game of catch with my friend Tommy from across the street. Or maybe we'd set up the street-hockey nets and get a game going. For street hockey, we'd set the nets up on opposite curbs of the street, and someone would yell "car!" whenever one would approach, interrupting the action as the driver, forced to slow down, would glare or in many cases give us the finger.

I was sitting on the front steps of Nana's brown triple-decker when Dad pulled up. I was the last stop. I got into the back seat and squished into the pile with the others, jamming my crumpled grocery bag under my feet, pushing Judy's knees out of the way in the process and against her protests. We were all excited, jostling and harassing each other for position as my father pulled away, anxious to get home and meet our newest sibling. We didn't make it one hundred yards before Dad slammed on the brakes and pulled over. Angrily, he threw the steering column shifter into park and turned sharply toward the back seat. Leaning in menacingly, he screamed at us all to "shut the fuck up" before someone's head got "knocked from its shoulders," one of his favorite expressions. That one, and of course, "I'll hit you with so many lefts, you'll beg me for a right!"

Something in his voice told me this wasn't just a usual rant at us, and we'd better be careful. This was a rage driven by something else, but I wouldn't learn what it was until, as with many other things, years later. But from the minute we got home that day, we knew something was up between Ma, Dad, and Diane, because all my mother and father did for a few days after was snap at each other in front of us and scream at each other behind their bedroom door. Diane just stayed in her room, crying or lying quiet. All we could do was fuss over the new baby, Susan, and shrug off whatever the hell was going on.

Things got back to "normal" after a tense week or so, but on some of those nights that week, Karen and I would listen to my father muttering to himself out back on the second story porch as we listened through a window we'd cracked open in the attic just above and behind him. He'd put one leg up on the middle porch rail, smoke cigarette after cigarette, and say things like, "I'm the best goddamn man she'll ever find" or "I'll fuckin show them neurotics." We couldn't hear most of what he'd say, but we giggled so loud at the fact that he was talking to himself that we were sure we'd be caught.

He also enjoyed carrying on his one-way conversations while sitting on the toilet. Over the years, from when we were little, we could hear his mumbling from outside the bathroom door. When we lived in the apartment in the Mission Hill projects, the bathroom door had an old-fashioned iron keyhole that when you looked through it lined up perfectly with the head and shoulders of anyone sitting on the toilet seat. One day we heard Dad in there muttering again, but this time he was louder than usual, and we couldn't resist taking turns watching him chain-smoking, talking to himself, and gesticulating while conducting his business in the bathroom. He was talking about some "asshole down at work," and how he had a good feeling about hitting the "fuckin numbah" that week and declaring what he'd do with the money, and commenting on many other topics of the day that may have been on his mind.

As we were trying to control our laughter, someone must have bumped against the door, because without warning my father's head snapped left, and it appeared as if he locked eyes with us, although all he could see was a dark keyhole. We all scattered to the back bedroom, slipping and sliding in our socks and laughing in hysterics at almost getting caught. From then on, the keyhole was jammed with tissue.

❧

"I got you some new stuff to try today at the store," I said to Ma. "Canned Spam, you know, the real stuff, not the crap we had to eat as kids. And I got you chocolate-covered graham crackers too. That way you get a treat as you loosen your bowels," I said smirking.

Jody poked her head out from the kitchen on hearing that, her hand over her mouth trying not to laugh out loud. My mother couldn't see as Jody pretended to put her finger down her throat before going back to putting away the groceries.

Although I'm not a big Freud guy, I do think maybe he was onto something with the unresolved anal stage thing, because my mother seemed to be stuck there or had at least been back to visit it for a while now. We covered that in an introductory course: "The anal stage is where pleasure focuses on bowel and bladder elimination—coping with demands for control." Maybe it's just part of getting old, but at this point in time, her main focus was on bodily functions below the waist, and she wasn't shy about sharing her challenges and maladies in that regard to anyone. Her constipation would often lead to panicky phone calls for dietary advice or to beg someone to get her prune juice so she could at least "break wind." She much preferred it when the prune choice helped her to do a bit more than that and her diapers became soiled, to give her more news to report with pride, along with the development of any new hemorrhoids.

She almost always requested tubes of KY Jelly and Preparation H when we shopped for her, and she went through these at a prodigious rate. I was afraid to find out how and why she used them, but I knew it was related to her obsession with matters of the toilet, so I avoided that conversation and just threw them in the shopping cart without question if they were on her list along with the adult diapers.

"Sounds good," she said in a bare whisper.

"What else is going on?" I asked.

"Same old shit, you know, alone 24-7, nobody gives a fuck."

"Ma, if no one cared, why would we be here?"

"Not you, honey, not you, you know that." Yes, I knew. Mighty Mike, the designated, hero, was "always a good boy."

"Did you hear from Diane today?" I said, changing the subject.

"Oh, she stopped by for her usual ten minutes and to bum twenty damn dollars off of me for gas and cigarettes. I only see her when she frigging wants something. I don't see anyone else. They all hate me, and I was nothing but a good mother to every one of you. You always had clean clothes every day, and I walked you kids everywhere! Everybody says all these horrible things happened. That's bullshit! Where was *I* when all these things happened?" she said, seeming genuinely puzzled, her voice drifting away.

That was the million-dollar question.

Poor Diane. She'd been my mother's emotional and psychological pack mule since she was about twelve years old, and Ma still knew just how to prod her to keep pulling the cart. As the oldest and female, she was the first to reach the age where my mother could start to pass off to her the parental duties she herself couldn't be expected to perform because of her "nerves." My mother's "nervousness," to me, was really the baton she used to orchestrate the complex composition that must have played over and over in her narcissistic mind—a siren's song that began as a lullaby to each of us that she sang into our ears, whispering "Take care of Ma" to cultivate our worry and guilt and "watch out for Dad" to turn him into our common enemy, as if he needed the help.

I remembered all the times she'd pretend to faint, going back to when we were very young. It might be to get my father to believe she was too ill for sex that night, or when he wasn't around to scare us into thinking she was about to die, leaving us alone and at his mercy, and what would we do then without her? We'd be petrified.

"So did Diane have anything to say?" I asked.

"Oh, yes. Besides the money, she wanted to know if she could have Dad's old recliner from the back spare bedroom. She doesn't have a pot to piss in."

"She wants that piece of crap? Let me go look at it."

"I don't give a shit. But I told her I had to ask you." Oh, yes, Mighty Mike must approve! Ever since I'd gotten a full power of attorney when Henry died to take care of her bills, house matters, etc., *all* decisions regarding her, the house, and its contents were now deferred to me, according to her. Wow! How would I ever manage such an empire?

"Be right back, Ma," I said and headed down the hallway toward the back bedroom, which was really being used as a storeroom. The doorknob was tacky with nicotine, like everything else in the house. The room was piled high with boxes of old clothes, Christmas lights and decorations, and a dusty doll collection. There were a couple of old wheelchairs that were folded and leaning against the wall. *She must be storing them for Loretta,* I thought.

I pulled a pile of musty quilts off of the recliner to take a look. It kind of jolted me to actually see it again after all these years. My father had died over thirty years earlier at the age of fifty-three, and why the hell she'd insisted on dragging this chair around with her was beyond me. Looking at the chair now, I almost expected to hear my father's ghost shout some sort of command as he always did from this, his throne of power.

I'm not exactly sure at what age I first heard him bellow, "Trudy, bring me a cup of Sanka, will ya?" or some other such demand from the comfort of this faux-leather duct-tape-covered "bahka-lounjah," as he called it. The reclining chair and its permanent mate, "Jerry," were pretty much a fixture in every living room of every place we had ever lived as far back as I could recall. King Georgie, as we sometimes called him because of the chair, had a penchant for naming his prized possessions like his car, and Jerry was among them.

Jerry was a metal ashtray stand shaped like a black horse's head, with a beautiful brass ring through its nose. I'm sure it wasn't real brass, but it was pretty heavy. I used to think of that ashtray stand as a sculpture, and I remember it as the closest thing to a piece of art we ever had in the house besides Mother's varnished driftwood clock with the hands that wound round the face of Jesus, with brittle palm leaves someone had given her from the previous Easter wedged behind it or the empty Avon decanters all over her dresser.

The clock still hung over her bed next to the nicotine-soaked tapestry of the Last Supper that I bought her at a bustling open-air market during my tour of duty in Italy in a little town called Ostuni back in the seventies. Even nonpracticing Catholics felt obligated to display the props of the faith.

The recliner had started out forest green, but over the years through so many moves it became more a splotchy battleship-gray-and-green checkerboard because of all the duct tape used to repair the tears. No matter what, like with his food, Georgie always made sure he had his own creature comforts. In addition to his constant cups of coffee, he was a chain-smoker, and if not yelling yet again for Trudy or one of my sisters to bring him a cup of coffee, he would yell to any one of us within his line of sight to "come empty Jerry," as he constantly filled the amber-colored ashtray to overflowing.

Jerry and the recliner were the centerpieces of Dad's world wherever we lived and where, from their placement in the living room, he ruled over his castle. Most weekdays, he'd come home from working the loading dock or carpentry shop, hang up his grey or green work shirt with "George" embroidered over its left pocket, head right to the television, turn on *Candlepins for Cash*, plunk down on the recliner, push it back, and light up. I guess Ma really did have a thing for men who wore shirts with embroidered name patches.

After settling in, he'd yell for a cup of coffee after lighting his filterless Camel (later on, when he went to a filtered cigarette, it'd be a Winston), then have one of us stand or sit by the television to change the channel on demand. Thank God those were the days of only five channels. It wouldn't be long before his eyes would start drooping, cigarette dangling from between his fingers. Whoever was on television duty would watch the head of ashes on the cigarette grow longer and longer as Georgie's head started to bob and he began to snore aloud, mouth drooping open. Then, being very quiet, we'd slip the ashtray out of the top of Jerry's head and hold it impatiently under Georgie's gradually spreading fingers until the cigarette fell safely into it.

We each learned early on to stay out of that chair or risk provoking his wrath for that egregious violation. Of course, we'd dare each other to get in the chair when he was at work or napping on his bed after falling asleep yet again, often with a dime-store porn novel spread open across his chest. The picture magazines in his nightstand drawer would become an adolescent treasure for me and my friends, but I wouldn't let them see those paperbacks with the back covers ripped off and their strange titles, like *First Mom, Then Sis*.

If anyone took a dare to sit in the chair, we'd hang the threat of tattling on them over their head for leverage later. Getting caught in the chair could bring any one of a number of different punishments, depending upon his mood. If you were lucky, it would only be a verbal assault peppered with profanities; if you weren't, you'd find yourself running for cover with Georgie in hot and furious pursuit, unbuckling his belt as he charged after you muttering curses.

Other transgressions, like whispering to each other after being sent to bed at six o'clock on one of those summer evenings while the sun was still shining, or making too much noise while washing the dishes, could easily propel him to make the unpredictable leap from verbal to physical assault. Keeping us off balance was one of his major sources of power. "The belt" was another of Georgie's trademarks, and he wielded it with athletic prowess. It was almost with awe that I'd watch him unbuckle the belt, grab it by the buckle with his right hand, and pull it off in a flourish with the elegance of Zorro. He'd then fold it in half, adjust a firm grip where the buckle met the tip, and then with a hearty, "Come here, you little bastard!"—or "you little bitch!" if that were the case—he'd seek his quarry. It was pretty comical, as long as it wasn't you he was chasing. We joked that you could get him huffing and puffing enough that he'd literally foam at the mouth, although it wasn't funny when he caught up with you and gave you extra for trying to get away from him in the first place.

He got hold of me once when I had no place to run or hide, mainly because my pants were around my ankles. It was somewhere around first or second grade, and I'd been regaling my sister Judy with exaggerated stories of all of the toys and books our teacher kept on the shelves in the cloakroom at the back of the classroom, and how we were free to take them home and borrow them anytime we wanted. Of course this wasn't true, and she teased me without mercy about what a liar I was. Finally, she dared me to prove it by bringing something home. She kept hounding me, so one afternoon, I slipped into the cloakroom on the way out and put a couple of those treasured Golden Books under my coat to prove her wrong.

It wasn't stealing, I rationalized like a seven-year-old would, because I'd bring them straight back to school the next day and nobody would ever know. I had chosen two of my favorites: a story about Robin Hood and his merry men and one full of pictures of jungle animals. I walked home, my heart pounding, and then with gusto waved them under Judy's nose upstairs in the bedroom. In a surprising and cruel twist of fate, she immediately went squealing to my mother that I'd stolen things from school. Of course, Ma made the obligatory "wait until your father gets home" pronouncement, so the expected dread set in.

With a sigh, I took my ill-gotten gains into the bathroom and sat on the toilet to try to at least distract myself with the books that had caused me so much trouble. My father came barging right in, his belt already raised high and poised to strike. With a swift yank on my wrist, he had me up on my feet, and he swung the belt hard across my bottom and the back of my thighs as I grabbed for my pants, hoping to pull them up with my free hand, while screaming for mercy. There, of course, wouldn't be any. I hated Judy for weeks after and looked on with a constant glaring anger as she stayed on her best behavior to avoid giving me any opportunity for paybacks as I nursed my welts.

We were always trying figure out ways to soften the blows once Georgie caught up with you. Sometimes just flopping around could make him miss. Grabbing at the belt stopped it in its tracks on the way down, although that just made him madder.

My two oldest sisters have permanent claim to pulling off probably the most ingenious ploy of all when it came to coming away from a belt beating with the least amount of damage—in this case, none! It was right after Christmas one year, and they had each received these life-size dolls from Globe Santa that looked more like linebackers than little girls. Globe Santa was a toy charity drive put on each Christmas by the Boston *Globe* newspaper to get donated new toys into the hands of underprivileged children. I guess we met the criteria, since they were the main source of anything to be found under our Christmas tree, along with our individual gifts from our respective godparents, who never let us down. Globe Santa even wrapped them and put your name on the tag, and each was hand-signed "From Santa."

I especially looked forward to getting my annual activity kit that was always on my wish list. I loved to draw and sketch, and the box was always full of beautiful colored pencils and a sharpener.

As my two oldest sisters remember it, they were whispering too loud after lights-out, and after a second warning, Georgie came clomping up the stairs toward their bedroom unbuckling his belt feverishly as he climbed. My sisters shared a bed, and in a flash they buried their dolls side by side under the pile of tattered heavy covers and positioned themselves directly beneath the bed, lined up with the dolls above.

With only the light from the stairway shining in, Georgie began wailing away at who he thought were my sisters, to the beat of his usual cadence of profanities. Right on cue, my sisters began kicking the bedsprings at approximately where the dolls' asses would be so it looked as though they were squirming around, and with their best muffled cries of "Please, Daddy, no!" kept up the kicking and wailing. They only stopped when he stopped, turning away and muttering, "Now shut the fuck up, the both of ya!" Biting their lips to keep from giggling, they lay still until his footsteps disappeared. Then they crawled back into bed and kissed their dolls.

The most memorable of my turns with the belt was in the summer of 1964—the year I made my First Communion. I wasn't quite so lucky as my sisters. We lived in Jamaica Plain on Green Street, and I loved going to church and catechism classes and the way it made me feel holy. I was thrilled when finally the Sunday came that I got to put on the white suit and shoes and walk with pride up the aisle at Our Lady of Lourdes church, hands clasped, to receive the Eucharist. My parents never went to church except for weddings or funerals, but they insisted that we all go every Sunday. I'm not sure why they cared about our spirituality when they neglected theirs, but I didn't care, because going to church made me feel safe, and it was full of goodness. I wore the suit all day feeling like a celebrity, and I got cards with money in them from relatives and ate candy and was very happy.

As I was getting dressed for school the next day, my mother poked her head into the room and said, "Wait, what are you doing? Put on your nice Communion clothes for school!"

I was mortified. She'd mentioned doing that the night before, but I'd pretended not to hear her. Proud as I was of making my First Communion and wearing that white suit, no way was I going to face the humiliation I knew would come from my fellow first-graders at public school if I showed up in it.

"But I don't want to wear it, Mommy!" I heard myself shout.

"That suit cost twenty dollars, so get your ass in it now!" she snapped back.

I didn't want to disobey, as after all, I had just taken a giant step closer to God by performing my first confession, reciting the Act of Contrition, and receiving the Eucharist. What could I do? Crying, I got dressed, grabbed my lunch bag that I knew contained a sandwich made with a thick-cut slab of government cheese with mustard, and slammed the door to the apartment on my way out. I had to walk up Green Street to where it intersected with Washington Street, then go up the iron steps, thick with layers of green paint, and cross over the pedestrian walkway that took you to the now long-gone El platform to catch the train, then down the stairs to the other side of the street to continue up Green toward the red brick school at the top of the hill. As I climbed the stairs, eyes red, I made up my mind that I'd just play hooky. I knew that was wrong, but I also knew every bully in school would seek me out if I showed up dressed that way.

Wandering around the neighborhood, I must have realized that I stuck out like a miniature Pat Boone wearing that white suit and those shoes, and that I couldn't do that all day. So, heart racing, I decided I'd just go home, and surely Mommy would understand. She wouldn't want me to get beat up at school, would she? I knew God wouldn't want that.

I trudged back up the stairs to the apartment and opened the door. My mother turned to me, looking stunned. "Just what the fuck do you think you're doing?" she demanded, cigarette smoke streaming from her nostrils.

"Please, Mommy, I don't want the other kids to tease me!" I said, pleading.

"Are you ashamed of being a damn Catholic? Is that it?" she sneered.

"No! But I just want to dress normal, that's all."

"Go change and stay in your room until your father gets home!"

Now the fear really set in. *Maybe she won't say anything,* I thought desperately. Although she always used that threat, she didn't always follow through. After all, wasn't it all of us against him? We'd hear them in their bedroom some nights and sometimes heard loud but muffled voices, and sometimes what sounded like her crying. Next day, she'd tell my sisters that it was awful, and she'd warn them all to "watch out" for their father, whatever that meant.

I heard him come into the apartment and he and my mother talking in the kitchen, although I couldn't make out a word of what they were saying. I was in my room when he came storming in. I faked left and went right and slipped around him, running to the living room, where I tripped over the hassock in my failed escape attempt, narrowly missing bumping my head on Jerry. I dropped to the floor and curled up in a defensive ball, readying myself for the first blow. He grabbed me roughly by the left wrist and held me in a semi-dangling position as I struggled, unable to break his grip with my other hand, another useless tactic, all the while writhing like a skinny fish on a hook. I could see my mother's silent shadow in the hallway just as he twisted me around.

"Come here, you little prick!" he bellowed.

"Please Daddy!" I begged. No use.

By the time he was finished (and exhausted), I had a series of striped welts that had raised themselves on an angle down my back. I remember going in the bathroom right after it happened and looking at them over my shoulder using my mother's makeup mirror and thinking how odd it was that they could be so red and yet not bleed. It was hot and humid the next day, and my mother made me wear a T-shirt to the MDC pool so that no one could see as I ran through the sprinkler; we weren't allowed in the pool itself because she was afraid of the water. But once the shirt got soaked, people saw the welts anyway, and I was embarrassed by their stares.

She stopped me by the front door as I was leaving. "You know your father cried about hitting you," she said.

Good. I wanted him to feel bad. I imagined him sobbing in the dark, sorry for what he did. He must have realized that no little boy would want to go to school dressed in a First Communion suit, and what was he thinking beating me over it? I then imagined him coming to my room to rub my head and tell me so and promise never to do it again. The image faded. I would have forgiven him in exchange for that. The way she said it, though, made me feel as if it was I who should reach out and somehow console him rather than the other way around.

I guess I never forgot that beating in particular, because making my First Communion was such a big deal to me. If he really did cry the way she said, it must have been because he was seeking her forgiveness, not mine. How else would he have gotten her to go into the bedroom that night and not lay on the couch with a wet facecloth on her forehead? Looking back, I could see how he had proven me correct later that evening when they went out and came home from shopping with Trudy clutching her latest treasure stuffed into the crinkled plastic bag from a trip to Zayre. This time, the bag contained a new pearly white blouse with ruffled puffy sleeves. It was just like the one she'd seen and admired this dancer wearing on the Lawrence Welk show the previous Saturday.

She held it up under her chin and spread the sleeves wide for us all to see, saying, "Isn't it pretty?" We showed vague interest as hope slipped away, as always, that there might be something in the bag for one of us.

Right before bed that night, I asked her, "Mommy, why didn't you stop him when he was hitting me so hard? I saw you watching."

She just looked at me with a blank expression and answered in what we had all come to know by then was her patented helpless tone. "But honey, what could I do?"

That was the same answer she gave whenever we asked why there was never anything for any of us in the Zayre bag.

CHAPTER 4

I shook the recliner from side to side to test it, to see if it really was literally being held together at this point only by the sticky gray duct tape. I didn't want Diane's grandkids jumping on it, as I knew they surely would, only to find themselves flung to the floor when the back of the chair snapped off or something. But to my surprise, the old throne was still pretty solid. Might even be a decent chair again if she could afford to get it reupholstered. The good news was, in its current condition, it would be a perfect complement to her apartment's hand-me-down garage-sale motif.

I shut the bedroom door with just the tips of my thumb and forefinger grabbing the knob and headed back down the hall to the kitchen to wash the tackiness from my hands. Jody was finishing up putting the groceries away, pushing on the freezer door with both hands trying to get it to close. She pushed so hard that a faded photo—one of those old Polaroids with the white border—slipped out from behind the previous year's magnetic Red Sox schedule that was plastered on the freezer door and drifted to the floor. It was probably taken with the same camera my father used to take pictures of my mother in the bedroom that she'd shown to my sisters when they were young, telling them what a pig he was for making her pose like that. But she nonetheless kept them hidden under her mattress in a sort of collection.

I picked up the photo and looked at the faded image of my brother Eddie's fourth-grade picture, and then I slid it back into place behind the magnet. His dirty blond hair was cut straight across at the bangs, and he was wearing a striped shirt and black horn-rimmed glasses and was missing a front tooth. He resembled a young Austin Powers. He was about fifty now and still housebound, living out his life in a bedroom at Diane's place in Dedham suffering from a severe case of obsessive compulsive disorder that had kept him paralyzed with ritual behavior and crippling agoraphobia for the last eight years. Poor guy was so afraid to leave the room some days that he'd just hide out there no matter how hungry he may have been or how badly he may have needed to use the bathroom.

If we'd only recognized the clear signs pointing to where he was headed, going as far back as when he was the age he was in that photo, we might have done something to prevent just how rotten things would turn out for him, although we were really just kids as well. My parents certainly didn't pay any attention to those signs, that's for sure; even if they had, I doubt it would have mattered much for the kid. In fact, they hardly paid attention to him at all once Susan was born and replaced him as the youngest, so maybe that was the start of it all, or at least a part of it.

When he was a kid, he'd often wake up screaming with night terrors or would come sleepwalking into the kitchen while we played cribbage around the kitchen table after the younger ones had been sent to bed. And there was that constant tic accompanied by a slight stutter, most noticeable when he was excited about something. His head would snap repeatedly to the right, his eyes squinting in unison as his bangs bounced in time against his forehead, his body sort of wiggling all over as he struggled for words. Ma always said he'd grow out of it and to pay it no mind, and my parents never took him to see a single doctor. Since I left for the military while still a teenager and was gone most of the time after that, it was quite a shock for me to see just how troubled he was during one of my trips back home.

It was in the fall of 1986, and I'd caught a military flight back to the states from Germany to visit for a week. I had been sent back there to Augsburg, just north of Munich, in 1983 to my old unit a couple of years after my father died. All you had to do was sit around on standby at the flight line terminal on the base and wait for the next available seat on whatever aircraft was manifested back to the states and closest to where you wanted to go, and it was a free ride. It was pretty cold being strapped against cargo netting in a jump seat on the C-130 that lumbered at thirty thousand feet westward into a headwind over the Atlantic toward Pease Air Force Base in New Hampshire, but the price was definitely more than right.

With Dad gone for five years at that point, only Eddie and Susan were still living at home with Ma, then in another new place in Roslindale on Florence Street on the second floor of a triple-decker just off of Hyde Park Avenue. It was within walking distance of a package store where I walked over to pick up a twelve-pack of Michelob and drank it in its entirety one night while watching a Red Sox game. After drinking potent German beer for the last couple of years, I found American beer to have a kick like Kool-Aid. Ma was aghast at my consumption and asked if I was an alcoholic. I started to explain about chemical tolerance, but she only got confused, so I just grinned at her and said, "Yup, and so is everyone in the military."

I slept on the couch, and the next morning I was awakened by the sound of the front door knob rattling in a very peculiar way. I was lying on my side, and I lifted my head a little to see over the green vase with the dusty yellow plastic tulips. I saw Eddie performing some version of what looked like the hully-gully in the doorway—one of those dances we'd all do at someone's wedding reception at the American Legion Hall or Italian–American Club.

Fascinated, I watched in silence as he grabbed the tarnished brass doorknob in his right hand, pulling the door ajar just enough for him to stick his left foot out into the musty hallway and tap his toes four times as he jiggled the doorknob furiously. He then switched his hand and foot and repeated this behavior, all the while counting aloud to himself "one, two, three, four, one two, three, four."

He repeated this pattern four times, twice on each side, and then on his final utterance of "four," he slipped sideways through the door, closing it sharply behind him, making sure he made no contact with anything. I was only a fledgling psychology student by night at the time, but I knew obsessive compulsive disorder when I saw it. It seemed to grow worse every year after that. He was steadfastly fearful of seeking the treatment he really needed and would go into a panic at the very thought of help or hospitalization.

He never had any close friends—and certainly and sadly no intimate relationships I was aware of. Years later, I tried to help him understand that OCD was among the easiest to cure on the list of anxiety disorders, but unfortunately, for whatever reason and despite all our encouragement, he chose to remain trapped inside his own distress, his days now more or less confined to a single room with the help of enablers who just didn't know what else to do.

When I was stationed in Massachusetts for my last tour of duty, I visited him once a week for six months to try to help him better understand and confront his disorder, but to no avail. His anxiety exerted its power over all attempts by anyone to help him, and it became clear that the only way he'd ever get to a better life would be to go out and get the professional help he needed but refused to get. All I could do was pray that he'd find the courage one day to take on the battle I knew he could win.

Back in Ma's kitchen, Jody turned to me and said, "She's got enough crap in there to feed an army," as she at last managed to get the freezer door fully shut. "If I see another frozen Salisbury steak dinner, I *am* going to puke."

"Me too," I replied, squirting green dish soap into my palm and scrubbing my hands together briskly under the almost scalding water. As usual, the feeling of wanting a shower as soon as possible after arriving at Ma's place began to creep in. Jody's hands were already red, so I knew she'd washed them at least twice since we got there. Being a nurse, she was extra cautious. We avoided surface contact with anything in the house as much as we could—and of course always kept hand sanitizer at the ready in the car for the ride home. We'd also divert Ma's attention from trying to get us to go down the hall to her bedroom for any reason for fear of a lone surviving bedbug somehow stowing away on one of our socks or something.

Washing her hands one last time, Jody said over her shoulder, "I'm going next door to chat with the neighbor. Gosh, I forget her name. She's outside with her new baby, and I've been dying to see him. Did you see all that red hair?" Lowering her voice, she added, "Give you and Miss Sunshine a chance to talk."

"That's it. Abandon ship," I said, sighing.

"Oh, c'mon, just listen to her same old crap for a few minutes, and we'll be on our way to a martini and a fried clam plate. Yum."

Jody descended the short flight of stairs to the front door, and I heard her say, "See you, Mum," just as the screen slammed and she headed next door, leaving me to rejoin the pity party I knew my mother was throwing for herself in the other room. I walked back to the living room and resumed my position on the edge of the arm of the couch.

The Game Show Network was now on the television showing old reruns of *The Match Game*. The audience was laughing. I glanced up to see

Gene Rayburn holding a skinny two-foot microphone, and he had just said something funny to Charles Nelson Reilly, who was pushing his oversized glasses up on his nose with a long pointy finger. By the flowery shirt he was wearing, it had to be an episode from the mid-seventies.

Other than *Days of Our Lives*, the Game Show Network was the only channel Ma ever watched, except for when the Boston Bruins or Red Sox were playing. She'd call me up ten times on the day of a game to make sure she had the time right and knew what channel to turn to so she didn't miss it. Her enjoyment at watching those teams was really the only thing we had in common, and it at least gave us something to talk about besides her personal soap opera or her bowels. The channel that carried the Red Sox would often replay a game from the night before for those who had missed it. They called it "Sox in Two."

Even though she'd seen the original broadcast, Ma would sometimes watch the replay of the game, and when next we spoke on the phone, she'd say, "Did you see the game today? It was the same score as yesterday!" I gave up trying to explain it to her; she'd always insist, "No, no, it was a brand new game!"

"Remember, I had a shirt just like that?" I said, referring to Charles Nelson Reilly. Dad hated it or anything else that made any of us kids look like "dirty hippies."

"Oh, yes, I remember it," she said. "Your father didn't want you to have it, but I made him let you get it. Wasn't it for back-to-school? We got it at Bradlees."

"Yeah, I think so. No, you didn't make him get it, you bought it using your sneakies, remember? Then we told Dad Aunt Kay bought it for me." I detected a tiny smirk at the old reference to one of her secret successes.

"So what do you think about that chair for Diane?" Ma asked.

"Sure, if she really wants it, who cares? I'll bring my truck down next time and bring it to her if she can wait that long. She'll have to get someone to get it up the stairs to her place, though. I'll give her a call later."

"Oh, don't worry, she'll wait for anything that's free," Ma said bitterly, conveniently ignoring the fact that anything she ever owned herself had come to her free.

"Why do you have to be so nasty, Ma?" I asked. "Diane does more for you than anyone, and only God knows why. You should be glad to help her out when you can. She runs all over creation for you, getting your pills, picking up orange juice or whatever, coming over anytime you have a meltdown over dead batteries in the remote or a smoke alarm that won't shut off. She just came by last week to plunge your toilet, for crying out loud. You should be grateful!"

I always tried to speak in a calm voice, as though to a child, in dealing with her, but this time my tone was firm and a little angry. God, she was relentless.

"*I'm* the mother and an old lady! My kids *should* do things for me," she insisted. "What did I ever do to them?" she asked, indignant, starting to sob like a spoiled child and for no apparent reason.

Here we go again about "her kids," I thought. Freud ran through my mind. *She's demonstrating regressive behavior as a defense mechanism for being remonstrated for her selfishness and narcissistic personality.* She'd never understand that her bitterness toward being "abandoned" by her own children was more than matched by their disdain for her.

What she also didn't fully realize was that although most of them had established a firm physical detachment from her, she still had a psychological grip over them to some extent, even as they lived out their lives at a distance, clinging to their anger and blaming her and Georgie for what they perceived as the irreparable damage those two had done in corrupting our childhoods in every way. It really wouldn't have mattered to her one way or the other, even if she were aware, because how others felt about anything was of little concern to her.

"Look," I said, now more controlled and trying to ignore her exaggerated weeping as her psychologist had instructed. "Diane's got a ton on her plate right now, you know that. Dealing with Eddie, and her own crazy health too! She just had three stents placed into her heart. She's a full-blown diabetic. She raised Loretta's kids, and now she's got her own son's kid to take care of. And she's sixty years old! You have to really try not to stress her out any more, Ma, okay?"

Diane was followed in the birth order by Judy, then me, Loretta, Karen, David, Eddie, and Susan. Susan was the outlier, having been born seven years after Eddie when we lived at that house on Walworth Street. We always called her the baby, well into her twenties. I have a framed, grainy, black-and-white picture taken sometime in the early sixties of all of us kids save Susan. Eddie was just an infant in Judy's arms, and we're standing in the living room with everyone smiling at the camera except me, standing there in the back, peeking out with a face too serious for a child and gazing right into the lens. We looked unexpectedly well-nourished and were just a little too young yet to understand the psychological and physical dangers already percolating in our midst.

These days, it was just Diane, Susan, and I who really had anything to do with Gert. As far as Judy was concerned, Ma was "dead to her," and she considered our aunt Esther to be her "real mother." Judy and I were the only ones to graduate high school, although some of the others went on to get their GED. She and I kind of lost touch after I joined the air force. She moved up north to New Hampshire to get away from anything to do with the family and to raise her own. She'd decided early on she'd head for the hills, and so she did.

Aunt Esther was one of my mother's five sisters, and she was everything my mother wasn't and we wished she was. We all looked forward to seeing our aunt and cousins. She was always laughing and was a working mother who made sure her kids were well-fed, happy, and full of life. Such a stark contrast to the world we lived in.

She once told Judy and I that when my mother was due to give birth to Eddie, Esther offered to take David, who was about two years old, to stay with her. We all got farmed out to other relatives, as usual whenever my mother was going into the hospital to give birth. I, as always, got to stay with Nana Bovaird, and I loved sleeping on the couch, listening to her cuckoo clock strike in the quiet morning hours. It was a gift from one of my uncles who'd been stationed in Germany with the army, much in the same way I'd brought one back for my mother.

Aunt Esther explained that when David was there, she was feeding him and some of my cousins their dinner. When she placed Dave in the high chair and put his dish on the tray, "he started to scream," she said, and "scared the shit out of me." My two young cousins looked at David with an odd expression but dug into their own plates with gusto. My aunt and my uncle Bud couldn't figure out what the hell was wrong with David. Uncle Bud pointed out to my aunt that David was staring at the pork chop on his plate and instructed her to take if off.

When she did, he stopped crying and went quiet, eating the potatoes, beans, and applesauce that remained on his plate. She surmised that the poor kid didn't know what meat was. She went into another room and cried. Later, when she was readying the kids for bed, she filled the kitchen sink and proceeded to bathe each of them one at a time. Her kids loved bath time and getting their hair washed. When it was David's turn, he screamed when she tried to put him in the water, so she sat him on the countertop and gave him a sponge bath.

She said it was the last time she took any one of us to stay over, saying it was just too distressing for her to see our reactions to a normal household. When my father came to get David and bring him home, she cried her eyes out and didn't want to give him back, but Uncle Bud said he wasn't her kid so she had to.

She was just a few years younger than my mother and had made her own way in the world, including earning her own retirement. She was determined and independent, unlike my mother, who was always dependent upon everyone else. Ma had a job for maybe two weeks in her entire life. Like my father, she never finished high school, but she did work for a very short time at the old Sears building in Kenmore Square, not too far from Fenway Park. She worked in the mail room and stuffed envelopes into pneumatic tubes destined for the various departments in the store along with the other girls. Then she met Georgie and had her eight children, almost all about a year apart, although there were a couple of miscarriages along the way.

My father, George William Boudreau, was born on September 8, 1927, to Angela (Boccuzzi) and Simon Aloysius Boudreau. They were living in the Mission Hill projects that sat at the foot of the Mission Hill district in the Roxbury section of Boston, in the shadow of the Mission Hill Church and its beautiful gothic spires. Technically, the church was elevated to a basilica status in 1956 by Pope Pius XII, and its full name is the Basilica and Shrine of our Lady of Perpetual Help, although everyone still calls it the Mission Hill Church.

I went to parochial school there for part of one year when we later lived in those same projects, and all the kids called it "Our Lady of Perpetual Motion," driving the nuns crazy. The Redemptionist Fathers first built it as a modest wooden mission church on the location in 1870. The present-day church was built in 1868 and made of Roxbury puddingstone, and its spires were added in 1910. Puddingstone played a historic role in the area, and there was a quarry that ran between Tremont Street and Allegany Street that produced the stone foundations of most of the late nineteenth-century houses in the surrounding neighborhood. The stained glass was exquisite and detailed and boasted the most brilliant colors, and there were dozens of abandoned crutches mounted above the altar in one of the cavernous apses to the left side of the main altar. All were left behind by those said to have experienced a healing miracle right there in the basilica.

Next to the Vatican itself, I'd never felt myself to be in a more holy place. So when we lived in those same Mission Hill projects ourselves for a short time during the late sixties, after we'd been evicted from a place in Roslindale, I often slipped off to five o'clock Mass on Saturday afternoons, even though I'd have to get up and go again on Sunday morning. Of all the benign and forgotten addresses over the many years and moves, 33 Plant Court would turn out to be the most indelible and impactful one for me. It was there that, as a ten-year-old boy, I first discovered a real sense of spirituality beyond my First Communion and gained a sense of understanding that, although there were many fears that would have to be overcome in life, somehow I would. I captured a sense of hope and optimism on Mission Hill that never left me.

George was the only son of eight children and the third oldest. The parents of his mother (our Nana Boudreau) were born in Sicily and immigrated to Boston, making her a first-generation American and us one-quarter Italian. My grandfather was pure French Canadian, his parents having moved to Boston from St. John, New Brunswick, with original roots in Richmond, Nova Scotia. He served in the army in World War I and was discharged in 1918. He died in 1955 before I was born, just as I assumed my mother's father had, since he was never mentioned. It turns out he died in 1968, never discussed and long-estranged from the family, so I never knew either of my grandfathers.

Dad's parents still lived in the Mission Hill projects at the time of his discharge following a short hitch in the Coast Guard during World War II, where he served as a cook in a ship's galley. He used to tell us he was an aerial gunner who "shot down those damn gooks," and we should have been there when his ship went through the Panama Canal to see such a sight as the locks being opened and closed, raising and lowering the massive grey hull. As it happened, I did end up actually seeing that engineering marvel during my travels with the air force.

We later learned he had merely cooked, and although he could technically be pressed into action as a gunner when it was all hands on deck in battle, the only action his ship ever saw was when it sailed on that training mission that took it down to Panama for a ride through the canal and back up to the Coast Guard station in Boston from which it was based. He wasn't quite the Admiral Nelson type as he had described himself in his stories, and I could more imagine him running the bars with the boys in safety back in Boston in the now long gone Scolley Square, then a mecca for servicemen, than being engaged in naval warfare.

There's a cracked black-and-white photo of him somewhere that shows him wearing one of the old-style peacoats, his hands stuffed into the side pockets, with a white Coast Guard cap cocked jauntily to one side, almost touching his eyebrow. He looked like a teenager. His face was thin and gaunt, and he was smiling, with a cigarette dangling almost straight down from the right corner of his mouth. His expression belied any of the dark thoughts that I assumed must already have been percolating in his mind. His thinness made me wonder if he'd had to eat a bit extra to make the weight to enlist in the military, just as I had.

When he met my mother in late 1950, he'd just come back to Boston from living in Texas for a while and moved back into that small apartment in the projects in Roxbury with his parents that, oddly enough, was just a few hundred yards from where we'd all later end up at 33 Plant Court. He spent the next few years bouncing from job to job, mostly as a laborer.

As a high-school dropout, he didn't have many skills beyond the cooking he'd learned in the ship's galley, but there were plenty of industrial jobs around at the time, so he ended up working at warehouses, loading docks, and factories in towns like Chelsea and Medford. One that for some reason I always remembered was way up in Lowell, about a forty-minute drive from Boston, at one of the now long-dormant brick factories with their spewing smokestacks.

Other than my mother dragging me along with her one December day in the early sixties for the long ride up Route 3 to pick up Dad from work, Lowell was foreign to kids like me from "JP," where we were now living following yet another eviction. To us, places like Lowell were populated by dangerous and territorial kids far from the sanctuary of our own friends and neighborhood. I couldn't say now where the factory was exactly, but I remember being amazed at all of the huge, beautiful brick buildings and the sense of strength that the city seemed to give off. It didn't look scary to me.

I sat in the back seat shivering, as the car heater had given out weeks before, and listening to my mother cursing that Dad was late getting off work and constantly muttering, "Where the hell is he?" Finally, just as it was getting dark, Dad came out from the heavy metal door by which we waited parked at the back of the building. The sky was steely, and the feel of snow to come was in the air, making the skyline look more white than gray in contrast to the bright red bricks of the factories.

Ma slid over to the passenger side of the Rambler's bench seat as Dad got in and took the wheel as he always did, not saying a word to either of us. Quickly we were back on Route 3, heading south as both of my parents blew cigarette smoke out of their cracked windows. As we drove, I remember thinking Lowell was nothing like I'd imagined it would be. I found it to be way more interesting than intimidating.

Once back in Boston, I didn't give Lowell another thought until 1990. I was stationed with the air force about fifty miles north of London and taking a creative writing class I'd chosen as an elective in pursuit of a bachelor's degree at night. The professor told us of his personal adventures with a band of dropout writers and poets, including a guy named Ken Kesey, who called themselves the Merry Pranksters. This led to more revelations about this revolutionary group of writers; an introduction to Jack Kerouac; and learning how the Mill City, as it was called, served as his muse for an impressive body of literary work. I sat in class thinking how it seemed impossible that, having been born less than an hour from Kerouac's very stomping grounds, I'd never heard of him, his book *On the Road*, and this phenomenon that came to be called the Beat Generation, of which I later learned he was a reluctant pioneer.

Reflecting on Lowell at that time, in a classroom a world away, I remembered Dad coming out of that factory door so long ago, and my mother and I sitting and shivering in the parked Rambler waiting, lost among the bricks. It was mid-September, and I was scheduled to take leave back in Boston in early October. I learned that Lowell had started holding a festival of a sort each fall to celebrate Kerouac, one of its most famous native sons. In spite of the constant moves my family had made in my childhood, none had reached as far as Lowell. Between the memory of that first trip to Lowell with my mother and all that I was now learning, I started to develop a connection I couldn't explain. I decided that now, some thirty years later, I'd include in my trip back home my second-ever ride up Route 3 to Lowell from Boston to see for myself what seemed to be this "holy ground" that could so inspire one soul to produce such a prodigious and poetic testimony to its very essence.

I read everything Kerouac I could before taking that trip, with hopes of making my time in Lowell as meaningful as possible as I retraced the streets, steps, and places prominent in his life and works. I parked my rented

Dodge in the lot designated for the Lowell visitor's center and found my way to the main entrance. It was a cold but brilliant and sunny day, and I felt excited and alive to be on this unexpected adventure, about to take my own Kerouac city tour. The visitor center was nestled among some of those old brick factories I'd seen so long ago, now repurposed to house it and what appeared to be apartments or condos. It was a treasure trove of Lowell history and had a wonderful collection of books for sale. I grabbed some free literature and a map and set out on my quest.

My first stop was to take a look at the Paradise Diner on Bridge Street, then I crossed the Merrimack River to snap a picture of Jack's birthplace on Lupine Road. I continued on for the next few hours visiting places and haunts I'd read about, including the Franco American School's Grotto, the Pawtucketville Social Club (where he played pool), and the Boot Mill Museum (to see what few items he'd left behind in this world, including his knapsack and typewriter). At every stop, there were others like me, or clusters of people on guided tours huddling up close to their guide, straining to hear. I eavesdropped when I could for any nuggets of information and ended my tour at Jack's gravesite at Edson Cemetery, where a group stood silently by as someone read from one of his works.

After listening for a few moments, I drifted back toward the car, reflecting on the last few amazing hours, and felt as if I'd discovered something for which I'd been searching but couldn't name—some connection. It came to me as part of a subtle feeling of déjà-vu and that sense of having been there before. It was something mystical but comforting and familiar. I'd moved so many times as a kid and now with the military, but none of those places made me feel as if I belonged there. Lowell somehow did. Standing by my car, I gave the cemetery one last long look as I said a silent prayer to Jack, and I felt a firmness in my feet as though they were taking root there, telling me with certainty I'd be back, little knowing that I'd end up attending graduate school there at UMASS so many years later.

Dad's last job, before he got sick, was in a carpentry shop at the loading dock for a company in Dedham, Hersey Inc., that built water meters—some as large as a small car and buried underground—where he served as shop steward. He led his crew in making wooden crates large and sturdy enough to ship those giant meters, and he relished his role as their union representative. The employees were also prodigious in trading porn magazines and dime store novels with each other.

He'd come home some nights and hold court at the kitchen table. In his toughest voice, he told us how he was handling this or that grievance on behalf of a fellow union member. "I'm the fucking shop steward, and I'll take 'em to the fuckin' judge!" he'd say, talking about management and slapping his palm on the table, flecks of spit coming from his toothless mouth. He always took his full upper and lower dentures out the minute he came home, and his cheeks would deflate like popped balloons, instantly aging him ten years. He'd wrap them in the snot-filled handkerchief he always kept stuffed in his back pocket. "They'll see who they're fuckin' wit!" he'd lisp.

Truth was, he was a blowhard who, when challenged, "had no lead in his pencil," as my old hockey coach used to say. There was a time we were out driving when I was in the fourth grade and he started swearing, his neck craned out the window, and honking his horn at the driver in front of us for what he thought was the guy cutting him off. The guy jammed on the brakes, ran back to my father's driver-side window, and caught him squarely on the side of the head with a thumping right hand as my father desperately cranked on the window handle trying to roll it up. Seeing my father had no fight in him, the guy just threw his head back and laughed as he walked away. I remember the lump on his head and the fear in my father's eyes as he drove away, pale and sweaty. Not exactly a lesson in manhood for me.

As Georgie was living with his parents, Ma was living on Elmwood Place up on the top of Mission Hill near Parker Street when they first met. Gertrude Janette Bovaird was nineteen and the fifth-oldest of Cecelia and Gordon Bovaird's children. She was sitting on the street-level stoop of the triple-decker where her family rented the top floor when Georgie came walking up with one of the Bonapaine sisters who lived two doors down and my mother hung around with.

In anticipation of the introduction, she'd gone to great lengths to make herself presentable by wearing her best twin set, consisting of a powder-blue sleeveless top, a matching cardigan sweater made from the same fabric, and a pair of capris. She twisted the string of her mother's borrowed pearls that hung around her neck between her thumb and forefinger as she feigned indifference at Dad's approach.

"Gert, here's the guy I was telling you about. He's a friend of my brother Jimmy," said Joanie Bonapaine, introducing them.

My mother was smitten by the tall, lanky, wavy-haired Georgie, and they sat there on the stoop talking for hours about her recent return from a visit to her relatives in Old Town, Maine (the only time she'd ever leave the state), and his adventures in Texas and his time in the military, even if it was only at the Coast Guard station in Boston's North End, about ten miles from where they sat. They started dating and were married less than a year later, when, according to Ma, Dad celebrated by tearing off her wedding dress and raping her on their wedding night, which was how she became pregnant with my sister, Diane, who came along in February 1952.

We'd all heard that one time and again. Many of us supposedly entered this world through violence performed against her. We used to joke that that it was hard to imagine raping the willing, but that was the story she whispered to everyone. It wasn't until we were all adults that we learned Dad had been married before and divorced somehow to a woman while in Texas, and that we had a half-brother we'd never know. I discovered this when I found his divorce papers in an old rusted lockbox my mother had hidden under her bed as I went through papers for her after Henry died.

We didn't know our half-brother's name, but my mother remembered October 1950 as the month in which he was believed to have been born. I did a little research and discovered a Robert Boudreau was born that same month and year in Boston, and coincidentally had been in the air force and stationed at the Pentagon at the same time as I was in the late nineties. This was three years after I'd left the Pentagon, and by the time I learned this, he'd already been retired from the military, so I didn't pursue it any further. If he was our long-lost sibling, I didn't want to drag him into our world.

By all accounts, even as a young child, Ma was well on her way to becoming a distinguished graduate from the school of learned helplessness. My aunts reported that like Loretta, she was fearful to the degree of ridiculousness sometimes and anxious all of the time, and she was picked on by her siblings for her constant whining and sniffling. For whatever reason, she developed what psychologists would describe as "a tendency to see one's life as managed by an external locus of control" as opposed to an internal locus of control, where people believe that what happens in life is mainly a result of their own internal and personal capacity. Trudy relinquished early on any awareness she may ever have had that she did have ultimate control over her life, obstacles or others be damned. It was all a matter of choice.

She went to great lengths to sustain that notion to the world, and as she gave birth along the way, she injected that idea in the most damaging ways to her children—the immediate effect of which was making everything seem impossible and undoable. Although unable or unwilling to take control of her own life, she focused her efforts on psychologically controlling her childrens'.

Ma was fearful and anxious, it seemed, about everything in the external world. Her fears included being near the ocean, going up elevators, heights, driving on the highway, riding up escalators, and any form of public transportation. So, for example, none of us learned to really swim until we left home, and those of us who were able had to learn how to overcome the trepidation of all those other crazy notions of hers. Some we conquered on our own, others with the help of various stable adults in our lives when we dared to venture out from her crazy clutches and go out into that dangerous external world.

I'm not sure exactly when it was that it first dawned on me that our parents were such a formidable threat to us—Dad for his unpredictable, violent, and abusive behavior and for moving us around from place to place so often we simply had no sense of a permanent home, and Ma for standing by, apparently unwilling or unable to stop it, plus her virulent attempts to infect us all with her neuroses. These were the obvious and immediate dangers, but none of us could know then that for some, there would be long-term effects years after the physical threat had passed.

Not long after me came Loretta. She was the acorn who fell closest to the maternal tree, and I guess Eddie only got about a foot further away. Loretta and I were Irish twins, with my birthday in December and hers the following November. George and Gert didn't take many nights off in the bedroom. Loretta was born premature, and almost from when she could walk and talk, she was timid, nervous, and quite afraid of her own shadow. Leaves blowing in the street would send her running home screaming and afraid they were "going to get her." The boogeyman was behind every door and under every bed. She clung to Ma, who did nothing to ease her severe separation anxiety whenever she left the house. We teased Loretta without mercy, as kids will do, so along with my parents she holds us also partially to blame for her psychological condition when talking to her psychiatrists as they work together to heal her particularly wounded inner child.

When it came time to go to school, Loretta would often have a meltdown. We'd just get her out the door to start the walk to whatever school we were now attending, and she'd stop and clutch the first chain-link fence we'd pass and resume her bawling and crying for Ma. Usually it was Diane who would succeed in prying Loretta's almost-bleeding fingers from the fence, and then we'd all turn around and walk her back home. Ma would yell at us every time and refuse to write us a note, since we'd of course by now be late, and turn us around at the door. Loretta would then be instructed to lie down with a facecloth while my mother made toast and tea, just as she would do for herself whenever she was having an anxiety attack.

Since Ma was a professional neurotic herself, over the years she used her daughter's vulnerability to try to mold Loretta into her likeness—a helpless victim of everything and everyone. It was no wonder Loretta began having her own regular fainting spells followed by lying down on the couch with a damp washcloth plastered to her forehead. This became a common sight. Ma would close the window shade just like she did whenever she herself was having a "nervous attack," telling Loretta, "Just lie still, like I do, and you'll get your mind back soon." She only made things worse for Loretta with her inexhaustible example of helplessness and laughable home remedies.

Ma was already on Valium and some other drugs, as she had been for years. It wouldn't be long before she had Loretta joining her pill parade. Poor Loretta went on to spend most of her waking hours in a semi-sedated state due to so many medications, and she soon found herself shuffling between group homes. She visited twice a week with her psychiatrist, who had most recently diagnosed her with dissociative identity disorder and was helping her to uncover her repressed memories about the time Dad "almost got her," and countless other traumas for which she couldn't be faulted for blaming my mother for making her feel unprotected.

Once, during a brief stay with Ma between moves, Loretta reported that one of her thirty-five or so alternate personalities—I think she said it was "Bob"—tried to convince her to walk down the hall at three in the morning and suffocate Ma with a pillow. She later explained that she somehow snapped out of it, because as she started to walk, trancelike, toward my mother's bedroom, she was awakened by her "core" personality. After she told some of us the story, we of course joked with her about messing with Bob's plan. She moved out the next week, saying her psychiatrist said she had to do so because her relationship with our mother was "toxic." Imagine that! Brilliant diagnosis, Dr. Obvious.

Many years earlier, I had gotten a phone call from my father while I was stationed at Fort Meade, Maryland, when Loretta was about twenty-one years old and had not yet fallen all the way into the unfortunate abyss. Dad was ranting about Loretta's imminent marriage to someone he referred to as a "nigger drug addict." Prior to my joining the air force, my household status with my parents, while always a little higher than my sisters', was that of just another of their rank and file parasitical offspring. Now I was some sort of authority figure in the family.

What I didn't know was that after I left, I was portrayed by my parents back home as the one and only shining hope of the family. I was suddenly the "good one" all of the others should look up to and admire and only imagine they could ever be. In their world, my graduating high school, starting a military profession, and earning a real paycheck was nothing short of laying a golden egg. They had by now acknowledged that I had brains, but even more important, I was earning money. I could clearly fix everything with my mind and my pay stub.

My parents took to saying things like, "Wait until Michael hears about this!" or "Michael will straighten you out when he gets home!" whenever my siblings found themselves in some sort of trouble. My father would show off a picture of me, skinny in my uniform, to the guys at work and was especially relentless with my brother David in his constant unfair criticisms and comparisons to me, which drove David crazy, as it would anyone. This inspired him to be the first to call me "Mighty Mike." So this phone call to Fort Meade was just another spotlight in the Gotham City sky calling for the Boudreau Batman.

"Calm down, Dad," I said, listening to his tirade and wondering, yet again, what he expected me to do about this latest alleged crisis. "She's an adult and free to make her own choices."

"Yeah, well, call her and tell her she's full of shit," he demanded. I could tell by his lisp that he wasn't wearing his dentures, and I could picture the spittle flying from the corners of his mouth.

"No, I'm not going to do anything, Dad. It's none of my business, so just please leave me out of it!"

"Yeah, well, fuck you too," he said and hung up on me. We didn't speak again for almost two years. I didn't care. Like always, he only called or wrote when he wanted something from me. The only letters directed to Mighty Mike from him while he was alive and I was in the military, starting in boot camp, were to ask for money to help pay his bills and put "food on the table." He'd send me one of his utility bills that was a couple of months overdue with a chicken-scratch note on it in pencil, begging me to pay it so "Ma won't freeze" or some such plea. These continued for years, even after I'd gotten married.

I'd just tear them up. *Hell with you both, freeze,* was how I felt. I had my own family to feed.

In the meantime, Loretta became pregnant twice, having two children in two years or so while her husband ran the streets and bars and struggled with drugs. Eventually, he ended up homeless, and he died a short few years later. It was then that Loretta began a sad spiral into a world of psychiatrists, prescription drugs, group homes, and unrelenting feelings of loneliness while Diane helped raise her kids. Whatever other reasons there may have been that had made things so difficult for Loretta, ultimately it was Ma and her haunting, whispering echo of the same message to her over and over that one's life can only be lived as seen through the narrow, dark lens of learned helplessness and emotional distress that was most detrimental.

It was a message so persistently delivered to her, and to all of us, over so many years that it left each of us in our own personal struggle to widen that aperture and realize just how much personal control we had over what we could become. When I think about the paralyzing effect my mother had on Loretta's emotional and social development and ultimately her happiness, I hear Kelly Clarkson's voice singing what could be the soundtrack of Loretta's life: "Because of you ... I am afraid."

CHAPTER 5

Karen came next in the birth order, and she and I were the closest, having established an unspoken alliance from our youngest years. I think it was because somehow we'd managed to find the humor in most everything, and we typically didn't take crap from anyone. That humor helped us to be maybe the strongest of the eight of us kids, although I'd use that description for any of us with at least a little grain of salt. Still, because we stood up for ourselves, we both had enough natural fight wired into us to not get easily pushed around.

Unlike my other sisters, Karen and to a large degree Judy seemed to have received some kind of psychological inoculation against my mother's attempts to lure them into taking a big gulp from her bubbling cauldron of neurotic tea—the one from which Diane and Loretta in particular would, unfortunately for them, be forced to slurp with abandon thanks to Ma's efforts.

In terms of helping manage Ma's chronic neediness, Karen would check in and help from time to time, but living up in Maine made it difficult. She'd always dreamt of settling there and finally made the move. For years before, she'd have nothing to do with the "nut bag" on Sanford Street, but mostly as a favor to me, she'd put her animosity aside and step in when she could in a clinical but unemotional way, which was many times even more beneficial.

Growing up, both of my parents knew that Karen was not easy prey. Ma would just let her run the streets, especially after she'd kicked Karen out of the house for the umpteenth time, and Georgie knew better than to include her in any of the incestuous fantasies with which he regaled my mother as they made those muffled noises in the middle of the night. Karen carved out a good life with her husband and her dogs near the beach in Maine, and I was happy for her. Sure, she had her own level of bitterness over the past, but she did not let it affect her life as much as most of the others had. It was Karen who picked me up at Logan airport in Boston when I came back home after getting unexpected news in mid-October 1980.

I was just pulling the muddy jeep into the parking bay on Flak Kaserne after a long rainy day in a convoy droning down the autobahn with my mobile squadron, the 6913th, as we returned to home base in Augsburg, Germany. We were at the end of a two-week deployment and were grateful to be back from our classified location near a forest just outside of Cologne. I was very much looking forward to a real shower and a bed more than six inches off of the ground. I cut the choke on the engine as I eyed the operations officer's approach. After a quick salute and welcome back, he said the first sergeant needed to see me right away and was waiting in his office.

"Yes, Mike, please have a seat," said the first sergeant. He handed me a telegram-like piece of paper sent by the Red Cross, as indicated by the distinctive logo on the heading. I did a quick scan down the yellow paper with the teletype print and saw "emergency surgery was performed two days ago" and "your return to home of record is necessary and urgent." The next day, I was high over the Atlantic, crammed in a middle seat at the back of a DC-8 that was shuttling soldiers, airmen, and their families back to "the World," as we called the States, and trying to sleep as a dozen or more babies cried nonstop, their ears popping.

Karen filled me in on what was going on during our drive from the airport to my parents' apartment—yet another home I'd never seen before. They now lived in a two-family duplex just off of Cummings Highway in Roslindale, near Fallon Field, where I'd gotten my first hit playing Babe Ruth baseball in an itchy woolen uniform with "Roche Brothers Butcher" embroidered across the front. It was a swinging bunt on a fastball I never even saw that trickled to the pitcher, the ball spinning so wildly he couldn't field it in time to throw me out. To me, it was as good as a hard shot up the middle, and I stood on first base, beaming.

That must put the moves at over a hundred by now, I mused as I sat in the passenger seat listening to Rick Springfield singing about "Jessie's Girl" on WRKO radio. Through the fog of jet lag, and as my sister began to give me the details, I noticed the trees were starting to turn to those amazing brilliant shades of red, orange, and gold. It was my favorite time of year in New England, and in spite of the reason for being there, it was great to be back home in Boston. The air rushing through the vents in the dashboard smelled fresh and familiar.

"Well, you know what a stubborn ass he is," Karen was saying. "He'd been feeling shitty and losing weight for weeks, then he woke up last week with skin yellow as baby shit. Ma had to call an ambulance because he wouldn't go the hospital on his own. They just sent him home day before yesterday." She said the jaundice had been so bad he could barely move.

"So what are the doctors saying?" I asked.

Without emotion, she said, "Pancreatic cancer. It's terminal."

"Wow. Nothing they can do?"

"Nope, it's inoperable. They sliced him open, sewed him up, and are giving him six months to a year, the bastard."

"Does he know?" I said in a voice more calm than I felt.

"Supposedly, but the crazy fuck keeps talking about going back to work." She pulled up at the curb in front of their place and let the car idle in park.

"Aren't you coming in?" I asked.

"Fuck no. Go get 'em, Mighty Mike," she smirked. Her bitterness, always on display, still ran deep and was not unexpected. In talking with her now, it seemed to me she didn't even really feel hate anymore as much as she just didn't care what happened to him.

"Pick me up in an hour then, okay?" I asked. "I'll take us to lunch at Papa Gino's in Cleary Square. Can't wait to get a couple of slices and a Coke. I'm starving." Papa Gino's was always among my first stops when I came home.

"You got it," Karen said.

I walked up the creaky porch steps, let myself in, and made my way down the quiet hall to what I supposed was the living room. I could see his Winston glowing in the dark from the silhouette of his throne in the corner of the room. Jerry was standing vigilant by his side, as always overflowing with butts smoked all the way down to the filters. "Fuck cancer," I'd come to learn was his message. Although it was only mid-afternoon, the window shades were down, adding even more to the sense of foreboding.

"Hey Dad," I said as I crossed the threshold into the living room and my eyes adjusted to the dark. Seeing it was me, he put down the cigarette and stubbed it out with one jab. Then he pushed himself up with both arms and stood feebly. His gauntness was startling. Seeing him this way, it seemed more like he had six days instead of maybe six months to live.

He had always been considered handsome and was constantly pulling a comb from his back pocket to pull his wavy black hair sharp to the right, creating a perfect and even part. He kept a "regular haircut" and always made me do the same when I was a kid. No "fucking hippies" would live in his house. I couldn't stand the foul-smelling hair tonic the barber would streak down my hair with both hands before parting it on the side with the sharp teeth of his comb, making it look exactly like Dad's. His hair was now almost totally silver and shaggy and no longer combed very well, although I could tell he was still trying.

He stood gingerly and looked at me with surprise. His baggy eyes were yellowed, fuzzy, and bloodshot. They were a little moist too, and his cheeks were collapsed in on his face like two deflated balloons. The effect was even more exaggerated by the fact that he wasn't wearing his dentures. We hugged awkwardly because I didn't know what else to do, and I could feel his bony spine through the flimsy blue plaid flannel robe.

I couldn't remember the last time we'd physically touched each other. His breath had the familiar strong smell of a mix of coffee and tobacco. I had to hide my shock at seeing him so deteriorated in just the five months since I'd left for Europe. It occurred to me now I'd noticed the night before I left that he seemed a little bit thin.

"How are you feeling, Dad?" was all I could muster as he settled back into the taped-up recliner while I pulled up a side chair and marveled at his unimaginable transformation from those days when all I saw him as was a merciless larger-than-life tyrant into now just a feeble shell of his former self. Seeing him this way made me realize he never really was larger than life at all; it only seemed that way.

"Ah, those fucking doctors put me through hell," he said. "Sticking needles all over the fucking place—nothing but a bunch of quacks!"

Unlike my mother, Dad had no sense of deference to any kind of authority. He had a special disdain for medical professionals and scoffed at anyone who didn't. "Fuckin' quacks" covered medical doctors and "fuckin' shrinks" covered the psychiatric profession—the one in which my mother was profoundly immersed, earning her the title "fuckin' neurotic."

Those of us kids—pretty much all of us, as it turned out—who went through staggered bouts of depression and emotional disorder during childhood got that label at one time or another as well. When I turned eleven, when we living in Mission Hill, I experienced what were explained to me as anxiety attacks when my mother finally took me to see someone at the Children's Hospital in Boston. I began having bouts of panic accompanied by a strange feeling of what I explained to the doctor as "floating outside of myself."

I became concerned when the counselor explained that what I was dealing with was a short bout of what she called "dissociative disorder," a term I came to better understand much later. But I relaxed when she told me that it was nothing to be alarmed about, and that, in fact, in my particular case and considering my family dynamics, it was quite a functional response to temporarily step outside of reality for a bit. I didn't really comprehend this, but I felt better at the reassurance.

As for my father's coping with the acceptance of his disease, it's said that most cancer patients lucky enough to have loving people around them do okay dealing with the loneliness and depression that accompanies it. I'm not sure how it must have been for Dad, since taking a look around it was easy to see that loving people were in short supply. Through the years, we had all considered our relationship, really more or less our coexistence, with our father as an "us against him" thing, and in the back of our minds as we watched him waste away, I think everyone believed that somehow his imminent death was like God's justice to us—payback time. Ding dong the devil would be dead, right? That is what everyone wanted, right? The suffering would then be over for everyone—most of all for our mother, right?

"So where's Ma?" I asked.

"Who the fuck knows and who cares?" he lisped, with bitterness in his voice and his eyes maybe even a little teary. "She's probably off picking up more of her fuckin' nutty pills at the CVS." That, of course, would mean Valium.

By all accounts, Ma had been doing the best she could to bathe and feed him in spite of his belligerence while enduring his constant insistence that he'll "fuckin' show 'em all" once he got back on his feet and on the job again. Of course, that would never happen.

"So when are you getting the fuck out of the army?" he asked. That was always one of his first questions whenever I came home.

"It's the air force, Dad, and I just reenlisted for another four years," I said. Joining the military as a career wasn't something I'd really planned, but I knew as the end of my first hitch was coming up that I had to do something—since I had no other real plan—or else I could still end up like him. Not an abusive bully, but for sure laboring at some minimum-wage job at the Westinghouse plant in Readville or some other dead-end factory existence.

There was nothing wrong with making a living that way, of course, but I wanted more than that for a life. Even more dangerous was the idea of being back home and thus immersed in the family circus. That was not only unthinkable but downright terrifying to me in many ways. No, I wasn't about to do anything but keep moving forward at as great a speed and distance as I could, and the air force was the way to do that.

Dad didn't know it, but my enlistment in the air force was set in motion when I left home at just fifteen after a fight with him. I ended up moving in with some of Diane's friends who all lived in communal fashion in a triple-decker in Jamaica Plain on a dead-end road just off of Green Street, on Greenley Place, not far from the apartment we'd lived in where I experienced that First Communion beating.

It was about two in the morning when the fight happened. We were living on Bradeen Street, a few streets down from Roslindale Square and just shy of the Jamaica Plain line near Forest Hills. I'd awakened, startled, to the sounds of my mother screaming something at him from the kitchen. I got up from the couch where I slept most nights, covered with a dirty sheet, and went into the kitchen. I saw her standing by the refrigerator with a skimpy robe pulled tight around her middle, glaring at him. What was the bastard up to now?

Before I could say anything, he turned and screamed at me in that lisp, spitting, "Get back to fucking bed, you little prick. This doesn't concern you!"

I don't know what they were fighting about, and I didn't really care. It just sounded like, from her screaming, that he was hitting her. So of course, I clicked into "protect Ma" mode. Maybe it was about some new perversion that even she didn't want to participate in, who knows. Either way, something inside me snapped when he yelled at me like that, and

I knew in that instant that this would be the last time he would push me around. Reaching down and getting the courage from somewhere, I erupted back, my voice trembling but louder than I'd ever heard it, "No, fuck you!" I couldn't believe I was hearing my own voice.

Things seemed to move in slow motion as he lunged toward me and, with both hands, shoved me in the chest harder than I expected and up against the refrigerator. He worked to pin me there with his left hand while trying to backhand me across the face with the other. I was in a full rage and blocked his arm at the wrist with ease, deflecting it away. I charged back toward him screaming, "I hate you! You're the prick!" I shoved him back in the chest with both of my hands, feeling both shocked and exhilarated but also scared at the rush of adrenalin from what I'd just done.

His expression was more stunned than angry. He let his arms go to his side as we stood there glaring at each other. All that was pent up inside me for so many years now fueled my anger and my strength, and I kept coming at him, wrapping my hands around his neck, tight as I could. Frightened by the ferocity I felt, I flung him off to the side, again with surprising ease, his hip bouncing off the kitchen table as he almost lost his balance. He recovered his footing and rubbed his neck with his right hand, seeming surprised at the sudden counterattack and trying to come back at me as my mother jumped between us, hysterical, pushing him back out of the kitchen a little too easily, it seemed to me, toward the bedroom. By now, some of my siblings were also up and in the hallway by the tiny kitchen, screaming for us to stop.

I could see his attempts to get around her and back at me were half-hearted, and that he had that same look on his face he did the day the man punched him in the head through the car window. My mother continued to coax him back into the bedroom, yelling at me to get out. I could see by his expression and the way he wouldn't look me in the face that he'd never have the nerve to raise a hand to me again. Those days were over.

I had to get away. I ran to the dilapidated black lacquered dresser in the hallway between the living room and the other bedrooms and snatched what clothes I could, stuffing them into a brown paper bag. Then I bundled it up and ran out to his screams of, "Get the fuck back here!" over my shoulder. I ran under the streetlamps of Hyde Park Avenue for about ten minutes and then slowed to a walk, not stopping until I reached Cleary Square. No one came after me.

I played hooky and spent the next day waiting outside a friend's house in Readville until he got home from school. I convinced him to let me sleep in the back seat of his beat up Pontiac Bonneville convertible until I could figure something out. I'd been there a couple of nights when Diane came looking and found me. She convinced me to come and stay with her and her new friends over near Green Street in Jamaica Plain, where they shared a flat. Not long thereafter, we all moved to another place in Cambridge, just behind Central Square.

I ended up staying there and commuting to school over at Hyde Park High via an unregistered 1965 Chevy Corvair I bought for fifty bucks from one of Diane's friends. It had a leaky exhaust that gave everyone who rode in it a splitting headache from the fumes, so we had to ride around all winter with the windows open. It was so small I had to let my hockey sticks hang out the window on the way to games.

I'd only sneak home to see Ma and everyone when Dad was at work, and I never slept another night under his roof. I didn't see him again until about a year later, when they had moved again, this time to River Street in Hyde Park, not far from Cleary Square. He hadn't once looked for or reached out to me from the moment I was out of his sight that night on Bradeen Street, which was just fine with me. I walked into the house one day to see Ma, and there he was at the kitchen table, chomping on sardines out of a can, taking them out one by one with his bare fingers and dropping them in exaggerated fashion into his toothless mouth as he made smacking noises.

He looked up at me and nodded, and with his mouth full, said "Hey pal" but avoided eye contact. Good; he was uncomfortable. I was a little nervous and wary about seeing him myself, but I knew I couldn't avoid him forever, so I had made the decision to stop by knowing he was home and by now harmless to me.

"Hey," I nodded back, and that signified our truce. I started stopping by some nights to see my siblings and would maybe play a few games of cribbage with him as the dialogue between us increased over time and the tension eased. We never spoke about what had happened that night in the kitchen on Bradeen Street.

My father had no passion for playing sports as I did, but he enjoyed games of all kinds, like canasta or cribbage. I wasn't much for most board games myself, but we both loved cribbage ever since he taught me to play when I was eight. Little did I know that his old wooden cribbage board with the ivory pegs that he'd picked up somewhere during his time in the military would serve years later as our main diversion from talking about the past or thinking about the present as he wasted away during the final weeks he had left on this earth.

So there I was, living with Diane and her friends, Vicky and Steve, a married couple her age she had met one night at the legendary Can Tab Lounge in Cambridge. They'd hang around there on weekends drinking Budweisers from the bottle, eating bar pizzas, and listening to great jazz music. They became very close, and it wasn't long before Diane and her kids had moved in with them. Her husband, Bob, was over in Okinawa serving in the Marine Corps, and she partied a lot while he was away. After his discharge, he came back and opened a sandwich shop. Poor guy died of a heart attack just a few years later, only in his thirties,.

After that, at one time or another, various of my brothers and sisters rotated moving in there as I had, and Vicky, as we'd come to appreciate, became a second mother to us. Hell, a real mother. She and Steven provided us with a safe place where there was always rock and roll, the occasional but supervised sixpack of beer, a lot of laughter, and of course, Vicky's famous pasta sauce with pepperoni chunks. She and Steven were two of the most generous people I've ever known, and they made a huge difference at a time when some of us really needed it most. This was especially true for David when the time came for him to make his own escape from my crazy parents. He and Vicky became very close, and he still calls her Mom and looks after her.

Even though I'd gone back to school when I was seventeen, I decided to quit, although I'd almost completed my junior year. I began plans to join the Marines in the fall. In my teenage mind. it was *screw Boston, screw my family.* Forced busing had turned the Boston public schools into very dangerous places, and no one was getting an education anyway between the riots in the streets, fights in the cafeterias, and rocks hurled at school buses. Even if I finished school, there would be no money for college unless I could scrounge a hockey scholarship at a state school—where, if I was lucky, I'd earn a third-rate associate's degree, and then what would I do for the next two years to pay to finish up a bachelor's? Would I even be considered good enough to play hockey in a higher division? I just felt like I had to make something happen, as it was obvious stuff wasn't just going to come to me.

I was on the high school hockey team—in spite of being, I'm sure, one of the scrawniest but scrappiest athletes in school history. I was actually pretty good at both hockey and baseball, but hockey was what I loved most and a sport I took to at once. I'd laced on a pair of worn-out hand-me-down no-name skates at the MDC rink in Hyde Park a mere four years before, but once on the ice, it was as if I was a baby thrown into a pool who started instinctively to swim. I'm not sure why, but I could just skate. I took to it so naturally that I made the varsity roster after only one year of honing my skills on the reedy ponds by the Fairview cemetery in Readville that would later turn out to be my parents' final resting place.

We'd play all day on the weekends and then into the evenings under the streetlights of the bridge that joined River Street to the nearby parkway until our toes became completely frozen. We played pickup games at the Bajko Metropolitan District Commission rink, where everyone would throw in five bucks apiece to rent the ice for a couple of hours after making up sides. It wasn't uncommon for us do this at three in the morning, since ice time was so scarce. In spite of just one year on my hockey résumé, in no time I became among the fastest skaters, with slick stick-handling ability and shooting skills to match, and people actually wanted me on their team along with the other first players chosen. I couldn't get enough time on the ice.

I discovered great joy in every smooth stride, the ice crunching under my blades, and in every crisp pass that I sent spinning up the ice or slamming off the boards, or in hearing the sound of the puck caroming of a goalpost with a loud clank. Each time I stepped onto the ice on the pond or at the rink, I felt untouchable, in spite of the physical play. It toughened me up; I wouldn't last long otherwise competing among the bigger and stronger kids, and no way would I allow myself to be run off the ice. I felt free to fly in a way I could never have imagined and was amazed at the abilities that God seemed to have just reached down and given me in such a swift and unexpected fashion when pretty much every other player on the team had been skating since the age of five or six and spent years developing in local youth hockey leagues the degree of skill that it normally took to become good enough to play in the tough Boston District high school leagues of the 1970s.

It was as though my feet, hands, and brain just knew how to do it. Although I might have looked on the outside every bit as confident as my skills and disposition seemed to imply, no one could see the self-doubt that haunted me as it had about everything I did up to that point in my life. It didn't matter that I kept repeating my on-ice success and that I was getting better all the time and that I'd fight anyone no matter how big and no matter how many times I may have lost because I had to. I had to fight not only because if you didn't you'd get no respect and you wouldn't last long, but to keep proving over and over to myself that I'd never be like him. No one was going to punch my face through a car window or anywhere else and get away with it.

Deep down, I felt something like a fraud, a Johnny-come-lately compared to all of those three-letter jocks, all of whom it seemed had a real hockey dad who drove them to the rink in a warm station wagon while mine had never even seen me play, never mind giving me a ride to the rink. They had the best skates and sticks, while I dragged an old army duffel bag full of smelly used equipment and a couple of cracked hockey sticks held together with tape onto a city trolley that would take me from Forest Hills Station to the stop on Huntington Avenue that was closest to the old and dilapidated Boston Arena, all alone.

I couldn't help but feel like an imposter. They were born rich and had some sort of pedigree, and I was a poor relative or some sort of charity case trying figure out how to use the silver the right way at a fancy dinner. Although I had a couple of close friends, I felt as if I wasn't one of them, however much we shared the same passion for the game and the dream to play college then maybe pro hockey one day. It was as though they had a résumé that I lacked, and I'd be found out and let go.

Coach had some faith that I could play college hockey, or even perhaps beyond, if I worked at my academics and got into the weight room for maybe one year at a junior college and bulked up a lot. Then, he said, who knows? Though Coach's prediction about my hockey future didn't quite come true, he did turn out to be the one who put my life on the right course. Hell, he helped save it.

It was July of 1974, in the summer between what would have been between my junior and senior years at Hyde Park High School if I hadn't quit. I had already signed up for a tentative hitch with the Marine Corps and was waiting to take a second physical and some other type of aptitude test. I couldn't imagine what in the hell the test could be for, when all I imagined they were going to do was shave my head and teach me how to pound my fellow Marines with pugil sticks and thrust a bayonet deep into the chest cavity of my fellow human beings. I couldn't wait. I went around humming the Marine Corps song. I loved their motto, *Semper Fi*, short for *Semper Fidelis*, meaning "always faithful." I liked the fact that only Marines got to say that and wear it with pride. The recruiter gave me a yellow-and-red T-shirt with those words printed across the front in bold red, but I knew I couldn't wear it until I'd earned it by completing basic training.

I was hanging out alone in Brigham's, stuffing down hamburgers and a milkshake. At five foot nine inches, I only weighed one-hundred and thirty-five pounds, and the recruiter said I'd need to be at least one-hundred and thirty-eight pounds to be accepted for final enlistment. It wasn't until my early twenties that I saw my height jump to almost six feet and add another forty-five pounds between the gym and the three squares a day I'd get from the military.

I was sitting in a booth facing the window and could see my hockey coach approaching from the center of Cleary Square. *That's strange*, I thought as he walked in. *He lives in East Boston. What the hell is he doing here?*

"Thought maybe I'd find you here," said Mr. Lewis. Brigham's was where a lot of the jocks hung out, both during and between school years, and he'd join us sometimes after a practice at the MDC rink for a bite or a frappé. My girlfriend worked there part-time, although she was now off duty, and she'd gave us freebies when her boss wasn't looking. I always opted for the butterscotch sundae with vanilla ice cream, extra syrup.

"Hey, Mr. Lewis, what's up?" I asked, puzzled.

"You, sport. You're what's up. Just what the hell do you think you're doing?" he said, sliding into the opposite side of the booth.

"Excuse me?" I replied, feigning innocence. I guessed he must have heard about the Marines, and I should have expected this, knowing him.

"What's this shit about quitting school and joining the service?"

"That's right, Coach," I told him, laying out my plan. "Home has nothing for me, and I know I'll never get a hockey scholarship with my grades. And this busing garbage sucks. I'll do my time and then go to college using the GI Bill when I get out."

"Oh, really?" he sighed. "Now how the hell are you going to go to college without a high school diploma?"

"Crap." I hadn't thought of that.

"You can always get your GED while you're in the service and hope a shit school will take you with that," he said, shaking his head. "But good luck with that."

He got me thinking. My lousy grades in high school really had nothing to do with my academic ability. I earned my failing grades by skipping class.

At that point in my life, I was pretty much angry all the time, it seemed. I was pissed off at my useless parents, angry with the turmoil at school, and fed up with my rotten and abscessed teeth that just hurt all the time.

The only time I felt any contentment at all was on the ice or at Mass, and I hadn't been there in a while. None of us kids had ever been taken to a dentist, but I figured the Marines would fix me up. I'd get free room and board and medical treatment. They would give me the chance to prove I wasn't destined to be an insecure, skinny kid who *might* make good someday. I would challenge every weakness I knew I had, both mentally and physically, and return a man in spite of no one, including my own father, ever helping to show me the way. I'd do it on my own. I could see myself coming home on leave in my crisp uniform, a proud and muscle-bound trained killer.

"Look, Mike, come back for senior year and play hockey. Then, if you still want to join the service or do something else, you can! Busing is easing up. Everyone sees that. You're only seventeen, so don't rush away your options."

Mr. Lewis picked up my check in spite of my protests. He took it to the cashier, paid, and headed for the exit. One hand on the door, he stopped and turned back toward me.

"Think about it, Mike. I'll work with the faculty so you can make up the ground you lost last year. If you're willing to work, they'll go for it. The admin offices are open all summer. Go reenroll." Then he walked out and back the way he came toward Cleary Square.

I watched him until he was gone from sight, then I slurped down the rest of my vanilla milkshake and felt the brain freeze coming on. I pushed the cold glass hard against my lower left jaw to try to numb a throbbing tooth. I could taste puss. I slid out of the booth, stood out in front of the restaurant, and spat a yellow wad onto the ground. Right would take me back to the center of Cleary Square and my bus stop. Left and River Street would wind me around past the municipal building and YMCA, down to Metropolitan Avenue and Hyde Park High School.

I turned left.

I moved in with family friends of my girlfriend's parents who lived two doors down from their house up on the hill on Maple Street across from the Most Precious Blood church. It was arranged under the provision that I went to school and did chores around the house, and with all of their support and encouragement, I graduated high school the following June.

My girlfriend's dad, although a former Marine himself who had served with the other tough-as-nails devil dogs of the "Frozen Chosin" during the Korean War, extolled to me the virtues of the high-tech training and much grander quality of life the air force could provide, so I switched gears from my Marine Corps commitment and, just one week after graduation, on Friday the thirteenth, flew off to Lackland Air Force Base in San Antonio, Texas, headed to basic training, my first-ever real dental treatment, and the wild blue yonder.

"Well, I'm glad you're home now," Dad said, startling me. I was taken aback a bit, as he'd never said anything like that to me before. Maybe he thought Mighty Mike could fix him too. Looking at him then, I felt my first sense of pity, for both of us—knowing he was going to die soon. Unexpected little pangs of regret and sadness came over me as I thought about all the years of not really knowing him and not having the kind of father to whom a son could turn in times of need, even if only for a ride to hockey practice or a game of catch. And sadness at being twenty-two years old and unable to conjure up even one happy memory to tell anyone about some special day we'd spent together when I was a kid like my air force buddies would always do on Father's Day.

He's the one dying, I thought, *so stop feeling sorry for yourself. He put food in your mouth and a roof over your head, didn't he? What more did you want?*

"Me too, Dad," I said. Me too.

CHAPTER 6

Mothers are all slightly insane.

—J. D. SALINGER

"Yes, I know. She's got her troubles, that one," Ma said, talking about Diane while dabbing her puffy eyes with a piece of balled-up old bathroom tissue that she then stuffed into the sleeve of her robe.

"Exactly right, Ma. Please just give her a break, okay?" I asked. I glanced out of the picture window, and from my vantage point, I could see the back of Jody's head, her pretty long dark hair bobbing on her shoulders as she spoke with the woman next door in her driveway.

In spite of my mother's phony half-hearted sympathy for her, Diane was the one the rest of us worried about most. She was a physical wreck, but that didn't stop Ma from calling her a dozen times a day to lament her own life and loneliness, and to complain about something or someone. She was relentless in her demands for Diane's time and attention, and she seemed to have no limit to the level of strain she was willing to exert upon her daughter. She'd call and plead with Diane to come over, crying and acting panicky, or beg her to go to the store for her, as she was almost out of orange juice or some other unnecessary necessity, wailing "Please help me!"

As frustrating as it was for Diane, she rarely could resist. My mother had galvanized her with guilt from such a very young age that I suppose she was too conditioned to do otherwise. Full of anger, she'd perform her duty by fetching the orange juice or whatever it was Ma needed and bring it by, only to have Ma say something like, "Oh, I forgot to tell you I needed bread too, would you mind going back out?" sending Diane spiraling into a rage. This scene was repeated at least every other week or so, and I'd get a call from Diane wanting to vent. They'd have a screaming match with Diane storming out as Trudy sobbed and begged her not to go, saying, "Please don't be mad at me!"

Ma would then call me blubbering, saying Diane had gotten mad at her "for no reason" and had screamed at her, and wasn't that elder abuse?

This was a question she'd also pose to a first responder on one of the many midnight rides that followed those occasions when she'd fake dizziness or an anxiety attack and press the emergency services button that was a fixture around her neck. She would do this after feeling particularly neglected or whenever some other family crisis such as, oh, I don't know, say a relative's death would take attention away from her.

I warned her after her last episode that if she pressed that button again and generated another needless early morning journey to the emergency room, she'd better plan on staying. I even packed a small red suitcase with some of her clothing and showed it to her as I placed it as a threat by the front door, where it still sits.

"See this suitcase? Push that thing again for no reason, and I'll be bringing it to you in the hospital so you'll have a change of clothes to wear on the way to assisted living!"

This was the only leverage we had to get her to stop her theatrics, but she knew it would never really happen. I'd promised her that as long as she was healthy enough to live alone in her own home, that's what would happen. She was fine physically. Although she had her psychological issues, she wasn't the one suffering from any of the effects of those. She left that to the rest of us to deal with.

"Oh no, please, please, don't put me *away*," she'd sob.

"Well, then cut the games out, Ma. You're healthy as a horse and you know it, and those ambulance rides cost over thirteen hundred bucks every time you do this!"

"But *I* don't have to pay, right?" she'd ask, no real concern in her voice. She knew she didn't. Medicare and CHAMPVA benefits saw to that. Between her husbands, her children, and the state and federal government, she never earned or paid for a damn thing on her own in her entire life.

She'd had at least six of these jaunts to the Faulkner Hospital in the last couple of years, all unnecessary as it would turn out, and all for attention, according to the doctors. She clung to the part of her fantasy, I guess, that saw all of her kids running to the hospital to "save Ma," just like she got them to run down the hall when they were children the minute she was thought to be in any distress.

On one of those bumpy joyrides, a concerned EMT asked if she'd been eating well. In a weak voice, she lied to him: "No. I don't see any of my children, and my refrigerator is empty most of the time. Maybe I could get Meals on Wheels, since my family doesn't help me?"

The next day, I got a call from Elder Services of Boston, and a concerned and accusatory social worker asked me if I was aware that my mother had been rushed to the hospital and that she was living alone, helpless, and hungry, and did I want to sign her up for Meals on Wheels? Ma used to receive those, but she kept piling them up like cordwood in her freezer because she'd never eat them and considered them "gahbage," just like Salisbury steak frozen dinners before the gravy was rinsed off of them. I had convinced her that there were truly more needy people out there across the city that would eat them, and since she had enough means to buy her own food, which she did anyway, she needed to stop getting them.

I set the social worker straight right away on everything and arranged a meeting at my mother's house for the following week, where I gave the woman a detailed etiology of Ma's histrionics. We spoke in front of my mother as if she wasn't even there, and the social worker said she'd spread the word to the Faulkner emergency medical personnel. I told her there was no need, as they already had her figured out as one of their "frequent flyers"—a term they used for people like her. Ma gave me a dirty look at hearing that but didn't say anything.

I shook my head thinking about my conversation with Diane after her latest meltdown with Ma. I could, of course, relate to what she was saying. For those of us still willing to have anything to do with the woman, it was just about impossible at any given time to prevent ourselves from wanting to rage inches from her face to get her to see that we saw through her, that we knew her behavior was contrived and purposeful, and that she had to admit it was her intention to escalate our blood pressure and emotions.

We were on the phone, and I was trying again to help Diane understand that it was more that Ma just could not, rather than would not, see the hurtful impact of her bitter personality and constant manipulations on those trying to help her and those she purported to love. I told my sister again how futile it was for any one of us to lose it and plunge into a meltdown or to cajole and plead with Ma to acknowledge something, anything, about her role in causing so much relational fracture.

"I know," Diane admitted. "But can't she just throw me one friggin' bone, ever, dammit?"

"Look, I hear you," I said. "But I don't think she's ever been sorry for anything. She's just too far gone, you know?"

"I know. I have to stop letting her get to me," Diane sighed into the phone.

"Exactly," I said, knowing that this was easier said than done and that we'd be having another conversation just like this one before too long.

I could picture Ma after Diane had stopped yelling and shouting at her, just sitting there, her face glazed over in a comic expression, like a dog watching television, her head cocked to one side with a look that said, *Are you the one that's crazy?* I had witnessed one of Diane's previous meltdowns and could only sigh as I watched the veins bulge then recede back into her neck and think what a waste of time it was to try to reason with a true narcissist. It just wasn't worth getting so worked up. I told Diane all that later, but it didn't seem to help her control her anger. Ma just made it so hard to ignore because of the bitterness that seemed to ooze from her pores and the way she seethed with resentfulness at the idea that anyone could have a life or interest that took any sort of priority over pandering to her constant and neurotic needs.

Material needs were not the real problem. We plied her with enough orange juice to wipe out the crop of the state of Florida, enough cigarettes to kill a small town, enough KY Jelly to lubricate an Amtrak railroad from coast to coast, and of course, enough diabetic test supplies to bleed out an elephant. Her real desire ran much deeper than any of that, and I sensed that in spite of anything she said about "I loved you kids," deep down she resented every single one of us for leaving her true desire for us all to circle back around her unfulfilled.

But as for poor Diane, in the early years she had been forced to be the one who saw to it that the rest of us kids were taken care of, in any way she could, when my mother couldn't or simply wouldn't. It wasn't just because she was the oldest; somehow, she had been made to internalize responsibility for the rest of us in some way, although she was still a child herself. She'd carried this inexplicable belief that she had to take care of everyone throughout her life.

At twelve years old, she'd make us dinner out of whatever she could scrape together, help us wash our clothes, and make sure we had something to eat for breakfast and school lunch every day. Even if it was just a bowl of thin Cream of Wheat in the morning and a peanut butter or cheese sandwich for lunch, we never left the house without at least something in our stomach and a little brown lunch bag in our hand. She'd use some of the few dollars she made once in a while babysitting to buy a package of cookies so we'd have a treat to look forward to. She'd even pick crab apples from a neighbor's yard. Every year going back to school, we'd beg our parents for a real lunch box with a thermos in it like most of the other kids had, in which they carried cold milk or hot tomato soup—maybe one decorated with the Jetsons or the Flintstones. But we never got one.

My mother would stay in bed most mornings, saying she was fighting her nerves or perhaps the usual headache brought on by another night of what she'd be sure to describe to all of us as some sort of sexual terror behind the bedroom door. Diane missed more and more school each year until she just dropped out by the tenth grade. Ma was always telling my sisters how horrible Dad had been to her after any given night in the bedroom and describing how she'd "just laid there" and let him do it, and how he forced her to put her mouth "down there."

It wasn't uncommon for her to do this while holding a conference in the bathroom. She'd seat herself on the toilet, and my sisters would line up on the edge of the tub facing her, mouths agape as she spoke. While most mothers' talks with their daughters were more focused on helping them to learn about life and how to cope with the pressures of growing up, only slowly unfolding the facts of life and womanhood, my mother's mother-daughter talks were of a different nature, and not of the nurturing kind, that's for sure.

It was during those bathroom talks, my sisters told me, that they learned many things from my mother that no child should ever see, hear, or know from a parent. One of the things Ma felt compelled to share with them was that my father had torn off her pretty white dress and raped her on their wedding night. But, of course, she said, "What could I do?"

To me, that particular story was nothing more than another example of the psychological weapons she deployed from her heavily stockpiled armory of emotional manipulation and aimed with accuracy at my sisters' already vulnerable psyches. It was insidious disclosures like these, with their sexual overtones, that Ma used to subtly and slyly weave over them a smothering blanket of guilt, sympathy for her, and fear when it came to my father and men in general. It strengthened their belief that they had to protect her from some constant threat of harm from Dad and to steadily build on their ever-growing fear and loathing for him.

I'm told a couple of Ma's other bathroom lectures to further my sisters' education included a demonstration on how to properly insert a diaphragm, even though she called herself a "good Catholic," and an explanation of one of her favorite tricks: "If you put just a little ketchup on a sanitary napkin, you can fake your period so a man won't want to have sex with you!" She told them that if it worked for her like a charm every time with a man like Georgie, it would work on any guy.

CHAPTER 7

"**H**ey," I said in an attempt to change the subject and distract Ma from her sniveling. "I spoke with Susan earlier, and she told me Aunt Betty called to check in on you? Wow, that's been quite a while, eh? How's she doing?"

Betty was one of only four of my mother's surviving siblings, all younger, and none of whom bothered with her much, especially Aunt Esther. Ma and Betty had kept in touch for many years, talking on the phone almost every day and visiting each other maybe once a week for tea and smokes and gossip. In spite of that, I'm not sure it could be said that they were very close. Either way, those visits had stopped years ago.

"Oh, she's not doing well at all," Ma said, failing to sound as sympathetic as she'd hoped. "She's on insulin, and big as a house, she says, and has a tough time driving with her bad eyes. She's probably going to lose one of her feet."

"Why don't you invite her over to visit? That'd be good for both of you, to catch up, right?" I suggested. "I mean, there are only you, her, Esther, Paul, and Evelyn left."

"I don't fuckin' hear from anybody!" she muttered, ignoring my suggestion and already moving on from any idea of visiting with Betty.

Talking about Aunt Betty made me think again of Nana Bovaird, who had lived out her last years living with Betty in Quincy before dying quietly, really stoically, at ninety-nine years old. Nana was famous in the family for her sewing and embroidery skills, and for making beautiful embroidered patchwork quilts that she gave out sparingly to favored members of the family. I was thrilled when she presented me with one when I came home on leave one year. Its individual squares were detailed and colorful, and displayed in intricate detail the state flower and bird for all fifty states. I keep it folded in perfect thirds across the bottom of my bed in the winter, ready to pull on its extra warmth during the cold nights.

Nana loved receiving the postcards I'd be sure to mail to her from exotic places around the world I'd traveled to while in the military, so I guess the blanket was her way of letting me know just how much she appreciated such a simple gesture from one of her scattered grandchildren. She pinned the postcards with scenes from places such as the Appian Way in Brindisi, Italy, or an aerial picture of Berlin, Germany, to the brittle plastic on the outside of an old and yellowed lampshade that sat on the cluttered end table next to her favorite rocking chair. She'd sit there, watch her Red Sox, and drink her glasses of Budweiser each game day right up until when she went to the hospital for the last time one month shy of her hundredth birthday.

Ma didn't show much emotion at the news of her mother's death. She simply announced to me that she'd be going to the wake but not the funeral because of her nerves. To set that stage, she stood in the receiving line during the wake with my aunts and uncles and sniffled as the parade of those who'd stopped by to pay respects filed by offering condolences. Most paused for an extra moment to provide her comfort because she seemed so upset and distraught, but I could only look over and smirk to myself, knowing that this was just another one of her performances meant to show how much this whole thing had affected her nerves. Of course, everyone would understand why she didn't appear at the funeral. She knew, to her delight, that all the unknowing and sympathetic people would later say at the reception that followed, "Did you see poor Gerty at the wake? It's all just too much for her to handle, poor thing."

Like my mother, Nana could hold a grudge against anyone she felt didn't give her the respect and attention she deserved or anyone she felt was misbehaving. But unlike my mother, Nana was strong-willed and self-sufficient. She didn't give a damn if family members ever came around, and I'm sure looking down now she doesn't care what Ma does one way or the other. Some might even say she was downright mean at times, but she was always kind to me. Cripes, with Nana's genes in my mother's favor, she just might beat some of her siblings' odds, and we could wind up putting up with her shtick for another twenty years—if we didn't die first.

$$\backsim$$

"So why don't you give Aunt Betty a call, Ma? I'll pick her up sometime if that'd help. I wouldn't mind," I said, not letting her off the subject.

"I will, maybe soon, once I'm not so nervous" she said, almost as a reflex. She wasn't nervous, and she didn't give a thought about seeing Betty or anyone else who couldn't do anything for her or who didn't mean anything to her in terms of her ability to manipulate them. In spite of her constant complaints of loneliness and neglect, there really wasn't any "company" that she wanted, other than getting her children back the way she once had them—not necessarily because she loved them and wanted their company, but more to control them and put them back into their roles as her fearful supporting cast.

Oh, sure, it was handy to use an Aunt Betty, a neighbor, or even a random stranger who might come to the door for a little sympathy from time to time, but that was fleeting satisfaction, like a quick high. Besides, if they hung around too long, she knew they'd see through her façade like the staff had done at the Faulkner Hospital, and that would never do. No, it was her scattered and scarred brood of children that she was desperate to reform into a doting circle at her feet.

Despite the fact that at this point, Trudy's life was distilled to being, for the most part, a solitary eighty-one-year-old, 115-pound, chain-smoking, finger-pricking ball of misery, she clung with delusional determination to the notion that somehow she could, she *would*, reclaim her former and rightful role as the planet around which all of her children orbited, just like they did way back when she could, with ease, pull them in as close as hostages through her powerful gravity of guilt, fear, and threats of abandonment.

Looking at her irrational beliefs and behavior now after all these years—so far removed from those long-lost but not forgotten days when we were all in her and Georgie's clutches amid the Spam, the cockroaches, the beatings, and the head-spinning number of places we lived—was it even possible for her to be as oblivious as she seemed to be now about the psychological carnage she and Georgie had committed, and for her to not understand that the power of her spells had long been broken?

There might be residual damage, but no one was coming back, at least not in the way she wanted. What the hell was in that woman's head? Although her psychiatrist explained that her behavior was a classic hallmark of borderline personality disorder (by now her official diagnosis), there *had* to be some sort of awareness on her part, but there seemed to be none. I suppose there couldn't be any because her disorder relied on an ability to induce that sense of fear, obligation, and guilt—all the things that she needed to feel—only in others

Assuming that God had widened the gate to heaven, He is the only one who knows now what went on in my father's head. Through it all, it was as if the two of them pecked at our psyches day after day, like the eagle that ravaged Prometheus's liver. They couldn't see, nor did they care, that although we were surviving each day, bitterness and resentment was building over the years. Their children were navigating through life, essentially blind, in a boat with no compass. Some had already fallen overboard and were flailing their arms for shore, while the rest were headed straight for the rocks, clinging together in a badly leaking boat.

If asked to explain how there can be any level of hatred and resentment directed at one's own parents, I'd say that with my father, it was rooted mostly in his unpredictable and impressive array, and creative use, of physical and psychological abuses. With Ma, it was her profound emotional weakness and calculated thievery of so much innocence and her grievous violation of the most sacred of trusts—the kind that should exist between a mother and child, the kind that says "I will always protect you," the kind that says "Don't worry" when you fear the dark, "Mommy's here and will never leave you and will keep you safe at all costs," rather than instead showing the boogeyman where you are hiding under the bed.

Maybe because she had repressed so much truth about herself, however she perceived it, for such a long time, somewhere along the way she galvanized in her mind that it was she who was the greatest of Georgie's (and of life's) victims and always had been. Being such, she couldn't believe she'd been anything but the best mother she could be under those abusive circumstances. Her narcissistic needs therefore trumped all others'.

It's possible that she had to use the classic psychoanalytical defense mechanism of repression to protect herself from something unthinkable, but that unconscious tactic had now morphed into a deeper, crazier way of thinking that allowed her to accommodate the idea that even the emotional blackmail of her own children was more than justified to satisfy her psychological and emotional needs. What trauma must she have experienced that shaped her personality and turned her into what she'd eventually become in her old age? It had to be something dark and painful; it usually was. Something had to be buried back there in her past. She was always vague when talking about her growing-up years, and my aunts and uncles weren't much help other than to shake their heads and say she'd always been the needy and neurotic one.

Personality theorists say that people develop and "become" through the forces of both nature and nurture. Nature means what is inherited biologically, while nurture is made up of everyone and everything we come in contact with in our environment; parents, peers, teachers, and television, to name a few. Each of us is the product of our own unique DNA and personal experiences, all triggered into motion and solidified by something as simple as a chemical imbalance or a chance meeting. Maybe that helps explain why in a family like mine, personal outcomes can range so widely among a brood of eight children.

People often asked "Where'd *you* come from?" after they learned about the wackier members of my family, particularly my parents. I used to think of myself as a kindred spirit with the character Marilyn on the old sixties television show *The Munsters*. In that household, the monsters were the normal ones, and she felt herself to be the odd one out—a feeling I understood.

I did learn that depression and anxiety ran way back through my mother's side of the family, and her own home life was dominated, at least in the early years, by an alcoholic father, although she never drank herself. By all accounts, Nana was a modest drinker and was not overtly affectionate with any of her children—any one of which could be physically or emotionally ostracized for any perceived grievance. It wasn't unusual when growing up to know that one of my aunts or uncles was estranged from her at any given time and had been for years.

One of my aunts once told me that Ma had come back very much changed after her teenage visit to see relatives in Old Town, Maine, one summer—the only trip she ever took out of state. It was as if something had happened up there, she said, that made Ma more anxious than ever and suddenly promiscuous. She was only seventeen. Did someone abuse her in some way? Might it have been an uncle or a cousin? Some stranger? Was she dragged into the woods by a band of marauding lumberjacks while picking blueberries? No one seemed to know what if anything happened that summer, or they wouldn't say if they did. She never talked about it, and it was shortly thereafter that she met Georgie.

"Well, the offer stands, Ma. Just let me know, okay? It's only a visit. What's to be nervous about?" I asked, putting in one more plug for a visit with Aunt Betty.

"It's my *kids* who should be here taking care of their mother!" she snapped at me again. "I was a good mother! Someday you'll find me dead in this fucking chair, and they can all go to hell!" She was fond of throwing out that comment anytime she was feeling extra bitter.

"Here we go again," I said with a sigh, not wanting to go there but starting to do so in spite of myself. "Ma, everything isn't as perfect as you remember it to be. We've talked about this so damn many times, and with your therapist too, you know that."

She became agitated and snarled at me. "You kids were always clean! My therapist says the past is the past!"

True enough, but in saying things like that to Ma, her therapist really only heard my mother's distorted version of the past. The therapist would suggest to me ways to bring my siblings into a dialogue with my mother to address old hurts and maybe build from that. Perhaps then everyone could let go and move on and get rid of some of the residual anger and resentment. But the therapist just didn't get it. My mother was incapable of being a positive part of any such efforts, even if people were willing, which they would never be. And no matter how much I tried to explain, the therapist could never understand that the past, in the minds of Trudy's kids, was a boiling pot of bubbling and volatile emotions that could not be easily cooled by the dulcet tones of any therapeutic advice anyone might give so many years later.

I tried to check myself, but still not able to resist, I slipped, stupidly, into therapist mode myself. If Jody had been there, she'd have cut me off, saying that she was hungry and it was time to get going.

"Yes, Ma, I know; the past is the past. But you've got to understand that things are the way they are precisely because the past *does* matter, no matter what the therapist might say. You told me that she said that everyone should be able to move on. She's right, but it's not that easy. And didn't she tell you that in dealing with the past, other people's memories matter, just like yours? You get that, don't you? Your memories are your own and they affect you, right?"

She only looked at me with a blank expression.

"It's the same for everyone else," I went on. "Those memories have a very big impact on all of us, and on our lives and our relationships— including the one we have with you. What I'm saying is, you can't expect everyone else to worry about and respect only *your* feelings when they don't believe you have ever once considered theirs. You have to understand and care about their feelings, get it? It's about empathy, Ma!"

This was maddening and stupid, and I was starting to get pissed off at myself because once again, I hadn't stuck to the script: dump the groceries, kiss her forehead, plop down her allowance, grab any mail, shoot the bull for a few minutes, kiss her forehead, then get the hell out of there. No sooner had the last words I'd said to her come out of my mouth than I remembered an article on personality disorder that I'd read in an issue of *Psychology Today*:

> Empathy is the action of understanding, being sensitive to, and vicariously experiencing the feelings, thoughts, and experience of another. For a number of reasons, showing empathy is problematic for people with borderline personality disorder, narcissistic personality disorder, or both. Those with BPD are so caught up in their own emotional tornados that your concerns get lost in the chaos.

Jeez, what an ass I was going down that hopeless road again with her. I'd been doing so well over the last few visits in not taking the bait and focusing only on what it was I could control when it came to her needs. That included the shopping, the banking, the bill-paying, the doctor's appointments, and above all, my own emotions. But here I was, doing it again, trying to reason with the unreasonable and feeling the familiar agitation that let me know it was almost time to get out of the "loony bin" for another two weeks.

"Well, I'll give David a call and see if he's ready to talk with you again, okay?" I said. "Would that make you feel better?"

For the better part of the twenty years after my father died, it was David who had stepped in to try to help Ma the most in terms of "taking care of things." I left for the air force when I was eighteen and he was only twelve, but he was eighteen in 1981 when I was reassigned near Boston during the final months of Dad's terminal illness. I was sent back to Germany a short time later, and David was left as the one to "take care of her" and the one my mother turned to with Mighty Mike on the lam in Europe. If her car needed a battery or the electricity was about to be cut off at her apartment, Dave would find a way to pay for it. He remembered her every birthday and lent her twenty dollars or more here and there, knowing he'd never get it back. He looked after her always, in spite of the relentless demands on his time and wallet, never seeming to hold a grudge for her part in not protecting him from Georgie over the years. It wasn't until later that he realized just how much she'd actually come between him and our father.

David was always a mischievous but good kid growing up. Our age difference was a bit too wide for us to hang around the neighborhoods together, but we'd toss a football or play some street hockey in the driveway now and again. Sometimes he'd start a fight with an older kid that I'd have to finish, but I didn't mind. He was always smart and had a quick tongue, so for that my father seemed to single him out for extra derision and verbal and physical abuse. Even though I'd left home at fifteen and on lousy terms, once I went into the air force and almost at once earned my newfound status as Mighty Mike, David was left behind to demonstrate to my parents just how much he could never measure up to me.

A popular kid, he'd spend his time hanging out under the hood of one of his buddies' father's car or helping them and their dad put up a deck in a backyard or to wallpaper and paint a room. They'd all treat David like a father or big brother, and along the way he developed and honed impressive skills, from plumbing to construction, of which I've always been envious. He was an amazing hustler, in a likable way, street-smart and daring with a great sense of humor, and he always found ways to make a few bucks.

Other than negative attention, my father never gave him much at all. And of course, it didn't help that my mother was right there to provide a constant wedge between them by looking to David to be her protector. By making Dad his obvious foil, she cleverly put him in an inherently adversarial relationship with his own father, Oedipus-style.

Dave ended up playing hooky more and more, finding easy mischief here and there, and then quitting school without graduating, although he was among the brightest students. I could only imagine that he had to have been drifting inside and couldn't see what meaning school could even have for him when no one seemed to care whether he even went or not, or what his future beyond might be. He did a short stint in the army, then came back home, married, and had children while managing a few small businesses of his own in Hyde Park.

Everyone in town knew my brother. I used to joke and call him "the mayor" because he was so well known and well connected. If you needed a lawyer, he'd make a quick call for you. Can't get a plumber on the weekend? No problem; he'd get someone there right away. He'd do anything for anybody and was well liked by everyone.

But even his patience with Ma and her relentless neediness had run out. As she always had since we were teenagers, she'd criticize and demean our girlfriends and boyfriends and later our spouses, for those of us who married, and she was always harsh toward David's wife with mean gossip and constant snide comments. That, coupled with the endless phone calls he'd receive from her begging for orange juice or in a panic over running out of diabetic test strips, was causing too much of a strain on him and his family, so he just checked out one day. He had no more to give her, and I couldn't blame him.

He called me after he'd made up his mind. "Fuck it, Mighty Mike. I'm done," he said flatly, and that was that. In truth, I couldn't believe he'd hung on as long as he had. We ourselves didn't talk much, with him involved in his businesses and doing a lot of volunteering assisting veterans across the state, and me living an hour away or so from Boston.

I glanced over to the bookcase where Ma kept a cluttered arrangement of family photographs in cheap frames to see if David's portrait—taken while at Fort Dix, New Jersey, during boot camp in the army—was still there next to mine taken during my basic training at Lackland Air Force Base in Texas back in 1975. Our features were hard to see through the thick layer of nicotine that coated the glass, but there we were: him in his green service cap and me in my dark blue one.

"Oh, would you?" Ma said to my offer of calling David, trying to sound hopeful. "I really miss him."

That's funny, I mused. She hadn't mentioned his name in months. But I wanted to catch up with him anyway, so I would give him a call and maybe grab lunch in Cleary Square before the month was out. Mighty Mike's treat.

CHAPTER 8

"**S**ure. I'll give him a call and see if I can get him to pick up," I told Ma. She had given up calling Dave long ago, because she knew he'd never pick up for her. God bless caller ID.

Lately, he'd been hard to reach. I'm sure he was getting tired of getting preached to whenever any of us mentioned that he really ought to give her a call at least once in a while or maybe check in on a holiday. I guess he felt he was through with her, at least for now, so he was keeping his distance. He'd more than earned the break.

"When was the last time you saw him?" I asked. Had to be over a year at least, I was thinking.

"Shit, I don't know," she said, sounding angry. "I just remember he stopped down the street at Johnny's Market and brought me some juice and a quarter pound of bologna, and that's the last I ever saw of him."

"Well, I hope they didn't recognize him," I said, half-laughing.

"Why?" she said. "What's that matter?"

"Ma, please. You don't remember that Dad left Johnny hanging like he did to so many other guys?"

Johnny Vaccaro's store was really named Marascio's Market after Johnny's father-in-law, who'd originally bought the place. It was the prototypical neighborhood "connah store" and just a couple of blocks from Ma's house, and it sat on the corner of River and Norton Streets, right across the street from Tommy's Car Wash. Probably fair to say that every family in every neighborhood in Boston always had their own corner store, and Johnny's was now Ma's—again.

It was owned by the Vaccaro family, which had lived in Readville, I imagined, for generations. Nowadays, the store was apparently managed by one of the children, since Johnny himself had become too old to do so, although I heard he kept a hand in and sat around a card table all day with a few cronies in a little room just off to the side of the main counter. I heard he'd worked up until just a couple of years before, still slicing and wrapping cold cuts behind the vintage deli counter with its case filled with all kinds of delicacies we rarely if ever got to enjoy—imported Parmesan cheese, balls of sweet and soft mozzarella, bright green olives, and my favorite, prosciutto di Parma. He was known around Boston and Readville as "the Sausage King," making it fresh every day, and he ran Mayor Menino's mayoral election-night parties for twenty years, making five hundred pounds of sausage for each event.

Years before, during the early seventies, when we lived just down the street on Edson Terrace, Johnny's was our corner store, and I could remember even then Johnny or someone else behind the counter handing me or one of my brothers or sisters countless packages of wrapped cold cuts, almost always bologna, although we'd sneak in a few slices of Genoa salami once in a while, and then writing the price right on the wrapping with a black Sharpie. He'd check us out at the register, where we added to our purchase other items like maybe a half-gallon of milk, a loaf of bread for sandwiches, and a couple of envelopes of Kool-Aid, like Goofy Grape. All of it on credit, of course. He'd write down each item on our family's ever-growing IOU that he kept along with any others in some kind of ledger or book. I remember he sometimes generously threw in a package of Oreos or Hydrox cookies at no charge especially for us kids.

"You tell your father to pay me next time, eh?" he'd sometimes say. Or, "You kids gotta eat more too, you tell your mother! And those teeth!" He'd even put Ma's Kotex pads on credit whenever she'd send one of us on a special trip to the store with a folded note telling us to "hand it to the man." I made sure I was scarce during her time of the month. Things were embarrassing enough already. Johnny was among the kindest and most generous people we'd ever known, and I could only imagine how many countless others like us he helped throughout his life.

Who knows how much money was owed to Johnny by the time we moved on from Edson Terrace to take up our next new residence and began to victimize another unsuspecting landlord and corner store proprietor? Although it wasn't our fault, we kids always felt guilty and conspiratorial about taking so much from these nice people over the years across so many neighborhoods. We hated to do it but didn't know what else we could do. It felt like shoplifting, but with the owner's permission.

Sometimes when I happened to stop into any of those corner stores still in business—and there are plenty—I'd "accidentally" include an extra ten- or twenty-dollar bill with my payment, leaving the money on the counter and telling the clerk to "keep the change." I knew I could never make full reparations, but I figured a little bit here and there couldn't hurt.

Dad himself would never go in person and make the arrangement for credit at whichever corner store happened to be ours at the time. Since Diane was the oldest, he'd write one of those folded notes and send her to the store with instructions to hand it to the "boss." That person would then call my father on the phone, where he'd be smooth-talked into believing he'd receive full restitution by the fifteenth of every month, no problem, from a grateful father who just needed a little help from time to time to make ends meet while feeding eight hungry kids and a sick wife.

Dad would stay true to his word for the first month or two, but like clockwork, that would erode, and we'd be sent to face the store owner and his mounting frustration, month by month. But who could deny food to skinny hungry kids with rotting teeth? After a few months of that, we knew that it wouldn't be long before we'd see the rented moving truck, so we'd start to stock up on empty cardboard boxes. We wouldn't get them from Johnny's or whichever was our corner store, though, so as not to tip them off. It was best to just disappear without warning.

Unfortunately, although they helped, those groceries we got on credit weren't nearly enough to bring sufficient food into the house for so many hungry stomachs. Since we were broke just about all of the time, we were forced with regularity to accept other, just as embarrassing means of provision. I came to hate the refrain of "we're broke" over and over again whenever any of us asked my parents for anything or if we complained of hunger pangs. I swore I'd never use it or allow it to be uttered in my own home, no matter what the budget might be, and I'd be damned sure to work as many jobs as necessary to never get to be called "broke" and get to the point where there were literally just coins in the house.

We came to expect that answer, whether it was the request for just a nickel to go buy some penny candy down the street or maybe the fifty cents it would take to pay for our own ice cream whenever we'd be invited along to take a ride to the ice cream stand in Walpole by a friend's family. We'd at once, but with politeness, defer the invitation, but our friends' parents would always insist that whichever one of us it was tag along and go with them to the Bubbling Brook on Route 109 on the Westwood-Walpole line.

They'd have all us kids go and sit at one of the picnic tables around back of the stand after taking our order, so at least we were spared having to watch them reach into their wallet on our behalf. I'd always ask for just one scoop of butter pecan, which I loved even though it hurt my teeth and I had to swallow the nuts whole, since I couldn't chew without pain. Inside, I wished for one of those giant banana splits with vanilla, chocolate, and strawberry ice cream drowning in hot chocolate sauce and topped with a mountain of whipped cream and maybe even some marshmallow too, but they cost $1.50.

Always pretty social, I not only made friends with others my age in my neighborhood who were dependent like us upon government food and also had to make one cheap pair of sneakers from the sale bin at Bradlees or Zayre last an entire year but also met lots of "normal" kids at school who lived blocks away in real houses that their parents owned, with fences, lawns, garages, and most important of all, full refrigerators and freezers.

I remember one such friend: a short, stocky Italian boy in the fourth grade named Pasqualino Giammarco. He'd occasionally invite me over to his house after school to play a game of catch or kick a soccer ball around in his neat and manicured backyard that was surrounded by a black wrought-iron fence with sharp tips. It would be a few hours yet until dinnertime, but I could already smell the deliciousness wafting from the kitchen where I knew Pasqualino's grandmother was concocting another Italian feast for his family. She had come to America from a small village near Naples ten years earlier to live with her son and daughter-in-law in, and she made sure she kept them, Pasqualino, and his six brothers and sisters well fed.

We'd play in the yard until the sun started to set and suppertime approached, and Pasqualino would often ask me to stay over to eat with them. Even though I'd be close to salivating at the odor of the pasta sauce or soup or whatever it was Nonna was cooking that was floating to my nostrils from the kitchen, and I knew I was going home to a dinner that would be something like white government rice mixed with watered-down cream of chicken soup, I'd hesitate and then decline, saying I had to go.

"Nah, thanks Pasqualino. I'd stay, but my father will kill me." I'd stayed over for supper a few times in the past, and Pasqualino couldn't have known that if I got found out, I could end up getting a beating for it.

"What, my food is no fucking good for you!" I could hear my father screaming at me as he raised and lowered the belt. "You get the fuck home for supper next time! What, do you think your shit is ice cream? My food is no good for you, Mister Better than Everyone?" Still, I was tempted to stay, despite the risk, because the sumptuous spread being put together inside that kitchen was worth it.

"C'mon," Pasqualino would insist. "Nonna told me to tell you to come in. We got plenty."

Nonna was how they referred to his grandmother, and she too was always commenting on how skinny I was. I hated being so thin compared to the other boys my age growing up, and I became sensitive and embarrassed whenever anyone pointed it out, although I know they said it mostly out of concern. From other kids, of course, it was a form of ridicule, and I'd often end up in a fight over it. I always wore long sleeves, sometimes in layers even in the heat of summer, to hide my puny arms; and of course, shorts were definitely out of the question.

"Nah," I said again. "Maybe next time. But thank your grandmother for me, okay?"

"Sure," he said. "But Nonna says to take this." He handed me a chewable red vitamin he'd pulled from his pocket.

"Thanks," I said, popping it in my mouth and tasting cherry. "See ya at school."

Then I'd dart from the yard and start pumping my spindly arms and legs as I'd race hard to get home before the streetlights came on and the rice and cream of chicken soup or some such delicacy turned to complete mush—or even worse, was maybe all gone already. I couldn't take eating another poop pie, as we called those peanut butter sandwiches.

The two meals we most looked forward to every year were Thanksgiving and Christmas dinners. That was because they both came courtesy of the local parish, which provided a complete turkey dinner with all the trimmings to families in need with the food they collected through donations during their holiday food drives. All one of us kids had to do was to go to the rectory, ring the doorbell, and tell the nun who opened the door that we were there to sign up for "holiday assistance."

Again, my sister Diane would be the one to perform this critical mission, with one or two of us younger kids in tow. That was one charity trip I didn't mind making. We chatted, excited, about the boxes of stuffing and the cans of cranberry sauce we'd be getting as we worked our way up the long walk to the rectory's steps. We always took a last look around to make sure none of the neighborhood kids caught us coming or going, because they'd tease us without mercy about being "charity cases." Most of them were full of crap, though, because without their own families filling out the same slip at the rectory that asked for their name, address, and how many children in the family, they too would be facing a table void of those treats we so eagerly anticipated. Even though the nuns knew better, pretty much every family put down on the slip that they had at least eight children in hopes of getting as big a bird as possible to ensure leftovers.

One important part of our family's food-supply system that did not involve the goodness of a stranger's heart was donations from sympathetic relatives, mostly from my mother's side, including Aunt Esther. All of my mother's sisters hated Georgie for his parental failures and his constant sexual innuendos and blatant overtures, and they considered my mother to be out of touch, neurotic, and needy. They were always concerned about our safety and our health. Like Aunt Esther, my Aunt Kay, who was my godmother, and our other Auntie Kay, my mother's sister-in-law, looked on in disgust as my parents hauled us around, house to house, apartment to apartment, school to school, in a pretty much constant state of hunger and physical and psychological disrepair.

Sometimes when the cupboards were bare and the corner store was no longer an option, my father would put my mother up to calling one of my aunts to try to borrow five or ten dollars until payday so that she could get us fed. Most often, rather than money, one of my aunts would come by with a box of food, saying my father would just gamble the money away playing his numbers or use most of it on himself to get a "spuckie" or a clam plate from the sub shop after maybe buying a box of Lipton chicken noodle soup and some saltine crackers, or maybe some oatmeal for us kids that we'd load up with government surplus sugar to get it to go down.

A "spuckie" was a reference, specific to Boston, to a submarine sandwich, and my father loved them above all other takeout food except for maybe a fried scallop or clam plate with the little paper cups of sour coleslaw and tartar sauce, plus French fries on the side. His favorite spuckie was pepper and egg, and it was so hard to resist the urge to take a bite whenever we were sent to fetch one for him. The guy at the sub shop would overload the roll with a mountain of steaming buttery scrambled eggs and sautéed green peppers, lightly sprinkled with salt and pepper—a perfect combination. We had to be sure to move fast to get it home while it was still warm, or Dad would be pissed.

"Did you get extra peppers like I told you?" he'd always say.

He'd sit at the kitchen table in his white T-shirt, legs crossed in his work pants and fagged-out slippers, to enjoy the feast. But first, he'd grab his snot-filled handkerchief from his back pocket and swipe it across the front of his mouth in one swift motion as, at the same time, he popped out and grabbed his upper and lower dentures and wrapped them into a clacking bundle he'd stuff deep into his back pocket.

We couldn't bear to watch him eat—not necessarily because we didn't have any for ourselves but more because of the manner in which he ate. We came up with the term "gum a spuckie" because that's pretty much what Dad had to do with those false teeth tucked away in his work pants pocket. Since he had no teeth in his mouth, he'd have to grind his gums ferociously from side to side to masticate the food into digestible bits, his jaws moving like pistons side-to-side, the lower one exaggerated first to the left and then to the right. Once the food was broken down enough, he'd switch to chomping straight up and down, his mouth smacking open and closed, until he could finally swallow. Sometimes he'd point the torn spuckie at one of us, and with egg on his chin and his mouth full, offer up a bite. Ah, no thanks, Dad.

Even now, when a couple of us are headed out to lunch, someone will say, "I'm starving. Let's go gum a spuckie," no matter where or what we were going to eat, as sort of a catch-all.

As for my aunts' "goodie bags," for us they would contain stuff like milk, bread, a brand-name cereal or two, canned soups like Campbell's, a jar of Ragu spaghetti sauce, a box of pasta, and if we were really lucky, a couple of Kraft macaroni-and-cheese dinners—heaven in a box. Sometimes they even brought along a plastic trash bag full of our some of our cousins' hand-me-down clothes. We could have used a few rolls of toilet paper too, but how could they know that?

My father would always stay out of sight in his bedroom when these care packages were dropped, leaving Ma to accept the donations like a grateful prisoner, eager to show her relatives how my father had us all living in such deplorable conditions, and what could she do? They'd ignore her pandering, hug us kids on the way out, and roll their eyes at Ma's usual promise that this would be the last time she'd bother them as they headed back out into the night and home to our cousins, who were waiting for them in their heated houses.

CHAPTER 9

Don't tell me my father was wrong. Let me tell you something, a father who made you is wrong? A father, the breadwinner of the house there? The man who goes out and busts his butt to keep a roof over your head and clothes on your back, you call him wrong? … Let me tell you something, you're supposed to love your father 'cause your father loves you. How can any man who loves you tell you anything that's wrong?

—ARCHIE BUNKER

Ma just gazed at me with a curious, hurt look. I guess the notion that my father could have run out on a bill was simply lost in the junk pile of the past, along with the other memories she didn't choose to hold on to.

"He did?" she asked, as if in disbelief.

"C'mon, Ma, really?" I scoffed. "I'll bet he owed Johnny the most! I'm sure the kid running the place was way too young to have recognized my brother or any of us now anyway." Even knowing that, I still avoided Johnny's out of guilt, I suppose, knowing that Johnny himself was still there.

"Well, David didn't say anything," she replied.

"Even if they did, you know Dave. He'd have them convinced that they overcharged *us* all those years, and they'd end up giving him money," I laughed.

A corner of Ma's mouth twitched in reflex as if about to smile, but she caught it and got it under control. She wasn't about to come out of character for a joke that weak, even though she knew it was true. Dave was a very smooth talker and very good at keeping his cool under pressure. He believed that sometimes the best place to hide was in plain sight.

That smooth-talking coolness was a trait he picked up in spades from my father, and it served him well, especially in his diverse business dealings, which often involved lawyers, business owners, and the like. He knew exactly when to give and take, to ebb and flow, and he didn't lose sight of the fact that you never push people too hard to achieve what you want. If you do it right, they'll more often than not go cheerfully in the direction you want them to while thinking it was their own idea. Sort of like mental jujitsu. Besides, Dave understood that you didn't want to burn any bridges. He treated people with respect.

My father, in contrast, mixed his impressive powers of persuasion with a healthy dash of false bravado, bluster, and deception to convince, cajole, or even bully his way to what he wanted. It didn't always work, as evidenced by the punch in the head he took that day out driving, but he easily batted over .500 during his fifty-three years on the planet, I'd say. He always took his chances with bluff and bluster; I'm sure he figured that since he moved around so much, in all likelihood he'd never have to reengage with one of his "marks." I remember one instance in particular when I was eleven years old where I got to see the master at work up close.

"Wanna take a ride when you're done?" Georgie said to me one Saturday morning.

It was April 1968, and I was just finishing up a bowl of soggy puffed wheat. Puffed wheat was always in abundance, courtesy of the United States government as part of that regular pallet of surplus food they'd provide to us each month or so. It came in giant clear plastic bags and was pretty ghastly stuff. It looked more like packing material than something as edible as cereal. We'd put off eating it as the very last option when the pantry became bare of what we used to call "real food." That was our euphemism for anything name-brand and not identified by generic bold black letters on a plain white label with words such as "flour," "cornmeal," or "raisins." The puffed wheat was made even more off-putting by the watered-down powdered milk we poured over it that was sponged up so completely it was like balancing a spoonful of cotton balls when you tried to eat it.

This was back at that bleak apartment in the Mission Hill projects at 33 Plant Court. *All in the Family* and the Eddie Jones show were my parents' and the nation's prime-time favorites, and James Brown and the Beatles dominated the AM radio. As I sat eating at the table in the cramped roach-infested kitchen, I could hear a familiar voice coming from the black-and-white television in the living room bellowing "I have a dream!" It had been a few days since his assassination in Memphis, Tennessee, and Dr. Martin Luther King Jr.'s words were being replayed all over the television and radio stations. At eleven years old, I found myself both incredibly sad and now fearful following that tragedy.

We'd lived in that apartment in Roxbury since our most recent eviction from the first floor of a triple-decker on Poplar Street in Roslindale. I had especially loved that place because it was just down the street from the new library in Roslindale Square, from where I borrowed books like *Johnny Tremain* and *The Red Badge of Courage* and spent countless hours reading on my top bunk at night with a flashlight or listening to the Bruins play hockey through the earphone of my old nine-volt transistor radio that was hidden under my pillow when I was supposed to be sleeping. I continued that practice once we'd moved to the projects in Roxbury.

I could hear the announcer, Bob Wilson I think it was, and his sidekick, color commentator Johnny Pierson, an ex-Bruin himself, calling the plays, his voice excited over the din of the crowd. "Here's Sanderson now gaining the blue line, a drop pass to Orr, Orr winds up and sends a shot through a screen. Scramble in front now, it's Esposito, to the backhand, he *scores!*" I'd then hear the Boston Garden public-address announcer give the scoring summary: "Boston goal by number seven, Phil Esposito, assists to number sixteen, Derek Sanderson, and numbah fowah, Bobby Ohwa." Some nights after the game was over, I'd lie awake for a while longer, staring out the window at the moon hovering above the distant trees and imagining myself skating with powerful strides across the freshly cleaned ice at the "Gah-den" and scoring a goal for the Boston Bruins someday.

We were one of only a handful of white families living in our section of the projects, including the Hallahan family, a large Irish brood who had the apartment directly across the hall from ours. Michael Hallahan was a red-headed eighteen-year-old and a pretty good-sized kid. My sister Diane had a crush on him, but she was only fourteen at the time. Mike would look out for us and seemed to have the respect of the other teenagers, most of them black, who gathered each night under the lights of the dingy basketball court for pickup games. They also seemed to consider him just another one of the guys, although a racial slur or two on both sides could be heard when the play got rough, which wasn't uncommon.

A short time after Dr. King's assassination, I was standing with the rowdy crowd that always gathered behind the chain-link fence of the basketball court watching the games. A fight broke out, and Mike was in the middle of it. Someone smashed him over the head with a beer bottle, and I remember my urge to vomit as I looked at him lying there on the court, almost convulsing, with his head split wide open and blood everywhere. A couple of guys were kicking him and calling him names like "cracker" as the ambulance and police sirens closed in. I had never seen a violent injury like that before. The gag reflex took over, and I broke into a cold sweat.

With the pall of Dr. King's assassination still fresh, things were tense, and the atmosphere of anger and aggression directed toward us whites in the projects was palpable. We were all nervous and wary. Just a few days before, I was chased home from school by a group of very angry black kids, although I'd done nothing to deserve their anger other than being white and crossing their path, I suppose. I had just turned the corner from the Mission Hill School toward Plant Court when I heard "Get that white motherfucker!" I ran around the corner of the first red brick apartment building, making it there a few seconds before the gang behind me could make the same turn. That allowed me the fraction of time I needed to dart sideways into the building through a side door and run the length of the main hallway to cut back through against the grain so that I would then be behind them and could run in the opposite direction.

When they turned the corner, it was as if I had vanished. They quickly figured out my maneuver and spotted me, but only as I was in the home stretch to reach Plant Court and sprint unmolested to safety. I raced into the flat, breathless, and slammed the door behind me. We lived on the first floor. The angry gang now gathered outside the living room window and began yelling for me to come out while shouting obscenities and racial slurs. I ducked behind the couch.

Finally, the yelling out front died down, and I crept on all fours to the window to see if the coast was clear. As I was inching my head up to take a peek, a soda bottle came crashing through the window above me. Shards of glass grazed my hands as I jumped back, leaving me with about a dozen small nicks. I heard fading cries of "fucking honkies!" as the group took off running and laughing.

My father came out of the bedroom where he'd been lying down reading. He'd been home for a few days, out of work with another bad back. By now, he had fraudulently signed up for and was receiving welfare, but he was still working as a laborer. According to him, it was "none of the state's fucking business." Yelling, he blamed me for getting chased and for the broken window. He angrily shoved me away from the pile of shattered glass.

I couldn't understand why those kids were blaming us when I believed that I was just as sad and angry about Dr. King's assassination as they were. I really couldn't understand why my parents had brought us here anyway. It was frightening now to be living in a neighborhood that just weeks before, when we'd drive anywhere near it, they'd bark at us to "lock those damn doors!" My oasis, the Mission Hill Church, was less than half a mile away, and I wanted desperately to run to its sanctuary. For me, those projects were like living in heaven and hell. I loved the church and school so much, but it was like crossing a minefield to get there and back.

I was in the sixth grade and attending parochial school for the first and only time. In those days, low-income families from the projects could send one child to the Mission Hill school tuition-free, and I was the lucky one. I loved wearing the maroon blazer and the way the nuns made sure we all had something to eat and that every child got a valentine no matter what on Valentine's Day. Going to that school and being in that church helped me start to believe that for sure, there was so much more out there beyond the bricks and the soot and the roaches and the constant hunger and fearfulness that hung over our dreary project apartment like a smothering blanket. Not everyone lived like this, I just knew it; my time at that church and in that school was telling me so. God had bigger plans. It gave me a stirring sense of anticipation that something good was to come of my life, and it left me hopeful, strangely thankful, and with some small sense of inner peace, in spite of how things appeared around me.

At school, we all had a special affection for one nun: Sister Mary Margaret. She was very old, at least to us. She was also very fair and kind, but the kids made fun of her anyway, as kids will always do. At the time, there was a horror show on television called *Chiller Theater* that played every Saturday night on Channel 38 in Boston. Its opening featured a skeleton's hand pointing out menacingly from a shrouded sleeve, much like the grim reaper's, while the narrator welcomed you to the show with ghoulish laughter and haunting music played in the background. Sister Mary's hands bore an unfortunate but remarkable resemblance to that creepy one as she pointed to the blackboard or emphasized a point in class, so the kids called her "Chiller" behind her back. Of course, it sounded more like "Chill-ah."

I loved listening to Sister Mary's voice—a slight, stern Irish brogue—as she taught Catechism or sang us songs or told us stories. Most of us would vie to stay after class to clap the erasers at the end of the school day for her. It didn't hurt that we'd usually get a reward of a candy bar or bag of potato chips.

One day, I was the lucky one chosen to stay after and clap the erasers. All of a sudden, Sister Mary turned to me and said, "Master Michael, I have a question for you."

"Yes, Sister Mary?" I said.

"Could ye perchance explain to me why, for heaven's sake, the children refer to me as a cello?" she asked, puzzled.

Yikes, I thought. *What do I do now?* I hated to lie, but one came to me automatically. "Well, Sister Mary," I began, "it's the way you talk." *I'll just go to confession*, I rationalized.

"Excuse me?" she said. "What do you mean?"

"Well, you have such a very nice accent that we all love listening to you talk and sing, so we think your voice sounds beautiful, like a musical instrument!" I said with what I hoped sounded like confidence, now that I was fully committed to the lie.

"Hmm. I see. Very well. Thank you, Master Michael." She smiled only slightly, but my answer seemed to satisfy her.

"You're welcome, Sister Mary," I replied. I've always wondered if she really knew and if I included that white lie in my next confession.

As anxious as those times were, it didn't much matter, because it was that one move my parents made to the Mission Hill projects that I look back on with ironic gratitude—not only for the budding hope for something better that began to rise inside me then but also because, serendipitously, it was there—at eleven years old, sitting in the pews of the Mission Hill church staring at the beams of light streaming through the stained-glass windows every Saturday or Sunday—that I first felt that deepest part of myself I later understood was my soul. I loved the cadence of the Mass, the music and the smell of incense and the ringing of the Sanctus bells as the priest prepared the parishioners to receive Communion. I focused hard on every word of the sermon, and I wondered if people were really trying to live their lives as the priest told us we should, because surely they would go to hell otherwise.

When my father asked me to take a ride that morning after breakfast, I answered, "Okay, sure," knowing his offer was more of a telling than an asking. Years later, in the military, we described that sort of offer as being "voluntold." As the eldest male, I was pretty much the only one of us kids who Georgie would let tag (really drag) along on occasion while he was running his "errands."

I used to call it "Georgie business." It might be a trip to the post office, where he'd come out with maybe a new Spiegel catalog or a bill or two that would go unpaid, or maybe a ride to wash Bessie or get gas. When he had a few bucks, he'd sometimes take the both of us to the counter at Woolworth's for a vanilla Coke and a tuna melt, but I wasn't allowed to tell my brothers and sisters. He'd pick up a copy of the *Record American* on the way home as well to see if he hit his numbers in the "nigger pool," as he called it. All I understood was that somehow the numbers in the race results from Suffolk Downs that were posted on the back page of the late edition of the daily paper were used by the bookies for gamblers to try their luck by guessing what the numbers and their sequence would be in advance of the results.

I suppose that these rides were in some way his attempt at a fatherly mentoring or bonding session. Between swearing at the other drivers, he'd offer me such pearls of wisdom as, "Make sure you change your socks every day—there's nothing more disgusting than dirty socks." I couldn't argue with that logic, of course, but owning more than two pairs would have made following his advice a bit easier.

Other life lessons included advising me to always keep a private roll of toilet paper stashed away to avoid having to use newspapers, and to always, always lock your car door when driving through black neighborhoods. These rides were also really the only times I spent alone with my father other than playing cribbage some nights at the kitchen table off and on over the years. He'd pull the playing cards and cribbage board from the kitchen cabinet and say, "Wanna play?" Of course, that meant "*I* want to play, so get your ass to the table."

Both the rides and the cribbage games were marked by stilted and shallow conversation, and both were void of anything that could cultivate any kind of emotional connection. He'd talk, or more like go on a profanity-laced ramble, and I'd listen. Dad avoided eye contact, having this habit of looking off to the side or even past you as he spoke. Other than that interaction, there were no games of catch with a football, no excitement at knowing that he was in the stands watching my baseball or hockey games, although I'd always look to see if he was there.

I'd look at him across the living room some nights when we were all gathered watching Ed Sullivan or something with the lights out, him in his recliner, us kids sprawled on the floor, and wonder as the television flickered shadows around the room how my own father could sometimes seem to be such a stranger to me, and if he ever thought likewise about me. I often wondered too, what kind of relationship my father might have had with my grandfather, who died before I was born. Dad never talked about his father much, other than to say that the man would never put up with the kind of "bullshit" that we kids nowadays pulled on him, but I do remember seeing him tearing up out of the corner of my eye one night when we were all sitting around the living room watching *The Dean Martin Show* and guest star Jim Nabors sang a slow and mournful rendition of "Oh My Papa." Dad was sitting in his recliner, feet up, and although his face was a bit hidden by his right hand, which propped his head up leaning to that side, I could tell he was crying by the way his chest was heaving up and down a little more than usual.

Actually, he did also reference his father whenever one of us got old enough for a paper route or a part-time minimum-wage job for a little spending money. "You put half that fucking paycheck on the kitchen table for room and board!" he'd demand. "Every damn payday! My father said there'd be no fucking free rides for able-bodied kids. I sure as hell didn't get one!"

"Hurry the fuck up," Dad was now saying. "It's gonna start raining, and I don't want to get caught riding around in Bessie in that shit." Like his ashtray, his car had a name. Bessie was a battleship-gray 1960 Chevrolet Impala with the conical red taillights and wide double fins, and she was Georgie's pride and joy. She was a real cream puff too. I wasn't sure how he could afford it. I remember hearing my mother complain about a loan shark, although I didn't know what that meant.

Georgie kept Bessie spotless year-round, and in the winter when it snowed, even in a blizzard, he'd have us outside in the howling and biting wind cleaning her off and digging her out every half hour, being extra careful not to scratch the paint. Should Georgie take Bessie out for a ride after we'd shoveled her out and the storm was over, we were ordered to either place a trash barrel on the empty space or to stand firm guard on the spot to prevent any usurpers from swooping in and seizing it, a practice that could almost get you shot in the city of Boston.

It was drizzling just a little when we left the apartment and walked past the quad and then the playground to the parking lot shared by Plant Court and the one next door. It was a humid and sticky day, and Dad complained about Bessie getting wet after he had just waxed her the day before. I wondered where we were going this time. A man in a brown leather jacket wearing a green plaid scully cap had come by the apartment the night before night and slipped my father a folded envelope through the chain-latched heavy metal door of our apartment, so I figured he must have hit his number from the day before and maybe the cash was burning a hole in his pocket, as it always did. Maybe we were going to get groceries! If so, I'd plead for a box of Captain Crunch with Crunchberries for me and my brothers and sisters, knowing he'd say "Ah, go ahead, what the fuck."

Dad eased the Chevy out of the parking lot and onto the side road leading to Huntington Avenue. Even though he was only forty years old, he drove like a nervous old man and always used the old-fashioned hand signals to indicate his turns, sticking his arm straight out to indicate a left turn or positioning his arm at a ninety-degree angle to indicate a right. He took a right just opposite Spar's Drugstore, spinning the steering wheel smartly in that direction while bracing the heel of his right hand, fingers spread, against the center top of the wheel, then let it go, causing the steering wheel to spin back on its own to the left and the wheels to straighten. It was one of his patented moves. We were headed north up Huntington Street toward Copley Square, so I knew he wasn't going to check the mail, since the post office was in the opposite direction.

The light rain had stopped now, and the sun was peeking out from behind the low fast-moving clouds, making the day feel a little steamier. I cracked my window, rolling it down a few inches. We hadn't gone far past the Museum of Fine Arts when Dad pulled over to the curb, stopping by a meter. We were just opposite the newly constructed Prudential Center, whose bottom floor was made up of stores, restaurants, a coffee shop, and a few small business offices. We checked the meter, and it still had almost an hour's worth of time left behind by someone else's dime. Dad pointed across the street, indicating that we were indeed headed over to those stores. We climbed the short flight of new granite stairs shiny from the rain and walked toward the well-lit storefront windows. He held his arm out, stopping us in front of Radio Shack.

"There it is—right the fuck there, just like the one in the paper your mother showed me," he said, pointing. It was then I realized the reason we were here was so Georgie could buy yet another treasure to appease my mother, to go along with her cheap jewelry and closet full of stretchy pants with the stirrups and other such tacky clothes. Since I couldn't know how much money he had in his pocket, I held out hope that maybe there'd be enough left over for him to take me for a vanilla Coke and tuna melt, let alone stop for any groceries.

The item on display was a portable stereo, with a big poster next to it on an easel that read: "All In One Portable Stereo Phonograph! Now only $99.88! Save $20.00!"

"Let's go in," Dad said. The store was just about empty, as it had just opened, and we made our way around the vacuum cleaners and the row of portable radios to get a better look. A salesman in a burgundy vest and khaki pants appeared as out of thin air off my father's elbow.

"May I help you, sir?" he asked with a smile.

"Fucking A," my father replied. "You can tell me about this Victrola here."

I winced at my father's rudeness, but the salesman didn't. *He must see assholes like this every day*, I supposed.

"Well," the salesman began, "this is a beauty. It's an Airline Solid State all-in-one portable stereophonic phonograph system. This baby does it all."

"Whaddya mean, 'does it all'?" my father said.

"Well, it's got a four-speaker stereo phonograph that reproduces lifelike sound through dual speaker systems, and it has a full-fidelity FM radio plus popular AM radio too. All in one compact portable!" the salesman said with pride.

"Yeah, what else does it have?" Dad said, getting more interested, although I knew none of what the guy was saying made any sense to him.

"In addition to the four speakers, it has a four-speed stereo phonograph with a drop-down automatic changer, an eleven-inch turntable, and a crystal cartridge with diamond and synthetic sapphire needles. And we offer a portable phonograph stand to go with the unit at a discounted price of only $12.95."

"Can I pay for it on time?" Dad asked.

"Certainly, sir! Only five dollars a month if you like!" the salesman said eagerly, sensing he was about to close a deal.

"I'll take it!" Dad said.

"Absolutely, sir! But I'll have to place it on order for you, since all we have left is this display model. They've been selling fast. Such a good deal!" said the salesman.

"Oh no, I don't want to order one. I want this one right here," Dad said, pointing at the stereo. It was clear the salesman was caught by surprise, as he started to stutter his apologies, saying, unfortunately, he couldn't do that.

"What do you mean, you can't do that? I know my rights!" my father said, menace rising in his voice. "You can't put something on display and say it's for sale and when a customer wants to buy it, tell them that they can't have it! I want to see your manager!"

"Sir, I am the manager," said the salesman. "And I wish I could help you."

"This is bullshit!" my father said, getting louder and attracting the attention of the other customers who had, by now, started to grow in numbers. "You advertised it, you sell it, goddammit!

I could see where Dad was going. He'd only resort to such quick bullying if he sensed an easy win, and this salesman was showing his nervousness.

"Look," Dad went on, "I got friends in the Boston police department and the Better Business Bureau, and I'll be down there first thing Monday morning to press charges of false advertisement and get you run out of business so fast your head will spin!"

The salesman stammered, and looking around, said, "Calm down, sir, please. Surely we can work something out."

"Yes, we can work out you selling me this frigging machine," Dad snapped quite loudly.

"Very well, sir. I'll see if I can find the original box and get you squared away," he said, resigned, eager to stop the stares.

"Good," Dad said. "And since it's a floor model, who the hell knows how many people have moved the arm all around and up and down and turned the frigging knobs? That's worth at least a 10 percent discount, don't you think?"

"Yes sir, it probably is," sighed the salesman.

"Oh, and one more thing," Dad pressed. "Why don't you throw in the stand for free, since this thing might be damaged for all I know, and I know there ain't no refunds for display models."

"Why not?" said the salesman, acting defeated as he walked away to the storage room to find the original box.

"See," Dad said victoriously as he loaded the boxes into the trunk of the Chevy, "that's fucking how you do it. He tried to beat me, the bastard!"

One thing Dad hated was getting beat. He preferred to be the one to do any and all beating.

"Remember," he went on. "*Always* tuck it to them before they tuck it to you!"

Yet another pearl of wisdom that he not only shared with me but had also now provided me with a live demonstration of courtesy of the poor store manager.

In an upbeat mood that night, Georgie stacked up the "Victrola" with a thick pile of scratchy 33 RPM albums by the likes of Dean Martin, Theresa Brewer, Eddy Arnold, and my mother's favorite, Tammy Wynette, and we made Jiffy Pop popcorn on the stove and drank real Coke that my father stopped and bought on the way home, and we all sat around the living room listening as my father crooned along from his recliner.

He had a portable reel-to-reel tape recorder with a small microphone, and we'd take turns theatrically performing into it, then play it back to listen to ourselves, giggling with hysterics as we ridiculed each other. As much as my mother tried to model herself after Tammy Wynette, my father seemed to do the same with Dean Martin. He even worked on combing his hair to look as much as he could like the famous Italian singer, although he denied it when Ma would tease him. Actually, he didn't sound too bad when he didn't try too hard to sound exactly the same as the original. Maybe a martini would have helped.

I was shaking my head at the memory, telling myself, *See, there were some good times, right?* when Ma's voice pulled me back with a bitter tone.

"You're right," she was saying. "That David could sell snow to a fucking Eskimo."

"Well, you know where he got that from," I said flatly, now back in the moment.

"You know what they say, like father, like son," she snapped in reply. "And *always* tuck it to them before they tuck it to you!"

Well, "they" say a lot of things, Ma, I thought, *and thank God "they" are not always right.*

CHAPTER 10

You are the bows from which your children
as living arrows are sent forth.

—KAHLIL GIBRAN

Paying no mind to her sarcastic tone—the one she always used when speaking of David—I replied, "That's true. In some ways, they really are a lot alike. When I see Dave coming up the street, I swear it's Dad sometimes by the way he walks. And when he used to smoke, he held his cigarette exactly the way Dad did, remember?"

"It was smoking that killed your father—and all that frigging coffee," Ma said derisively, ignoring my comment about Dave. She had seen some show on television not long after Dad died that talked about a link between pancreatic cancer and excessive coffee drinking and cigarette smoking, and she'd repeated this assertion in a matter-of-fact tone countless times since Dad died in 1981.

Other than the mechanics of their walking and smoking, David and Dad didn't have much in common, but they did share an eerie similarity in the way David had doted on my mother, just as my father always had, and in particular in the immediate years after Dad's death. Again, I was away for most of that period of time, so perhaps he felt the duty had fallen to him since Mighty Mike had escaped to far-flung places—that, along with my mother's expertise at inducing guilt in him at a level second only to what she inflicted upon Diane. But no matter how much Dave did for her, she hounded him without rest, spoke in mean terms about him behind his back, and was especially critical of and downright nasty toward him to his face at times. And of course, any woman in his life had worse coming to her.

Nothing was ever good enough, but Dave kept giving because, like me, he couldn't help but care. It was puzzling to me how she could be so quick to bad-mouth him after all he had done for her over those years. Of course, she always denigrated people behind their backs, no matter how much they might do for her, and Mighty Mike was no exception. That was just part of her and who she was. But no matter—David went the extra mile, and not only had he helped her with paying the bills or fixing things around the house, but he was also always giving some money to Diane or Eddie or whoever else in the family needed a hand for rent or gas or cigarettes or whatever.

I realized over time, of course, that what she was doing was treating David the same way she'd treated our father. But why? It was as though she'd turned him into a sort of replacement to Dad as her new tormentor, although he was nothing of the sort. This was important to her— critical to her ability to keep her "victim" status intact and to let the world know that although Georgie might now be gone, she was still under attack, and everyone still needed to step up and "take care of Ma."

Because we spent our childhood witnessing what we truly believed to be her suffering and victimization at Dad's hands, we'd always presumed that she in particular would at last be free when he died, but it turned out that's not what she was experiencing at all. She was never looking for any liberation from him or the anguish she wanted us all to believe he was causing her. No, it was more that she had dedicated herself to perfecting and sustaining her portrayal as a quivering pile of helplessness while carefully cultivating everyone's perception that Dad was a domestic terrorist to us all and she his most helpless victim. She couldn't allow the inconvenient fact that he was dead to change any of that.

So it turned out that all of her yearning-to-be-free performances of Tammy Wynette and Eddy Arnold songs were just more props in her play—a fitting soundtrack to the way she was telling the story. She needed to use David as her victimizer until a better option came along. It was really only the story that mattered to Ma, a story so important that, with her personality disorder, she could easily and without emotion kill off or write in or out of it any characters as necessary so long as she remained the unchanging protagonist, a perpetual damsel in distress who demanded never-ending attention through her attempts to put the ones she said she loved through a pathological cycle of fear, obligation, and guilt.

This theory of replacement tormentors solidified when she married

Henry. With astonishing quickness, she became detached from her neediness for David, because she now had a new, more appropriate and immediate subjugator living under her very own roof, a true stand-in for Dad who, although unfamiliar with the script of her lifelong drama, would nonetheless be thrust into the role of leading man in her own personal and distorted version of Beauty and the Beast. Of course, she hid her true plan from Henry, providing him with no clue of what lay ahead during those heady days of their courtship. But it soon became Henry who she hounded nonstop, talked behind the back of, and focused her harshest and meanest criticisms on. All this, of course, because of what he was "doing" to her—just what all the others before him had done.

I could only imagine that the transformation from courtship to constant antagonism and accusations was like a sucker punch to poor unsuspecting Henry. There were no more walks on the beach, no sunny afternoons at Fenway Park, no Irish jigs. And as everyone soon came to learn from her, there was definitely no sex. She continued to curse him for that long after he was gone. At least Georgie had never denied her that, although she "hated" every minute of it. All Henry had wanted was companionship in his old age. For what she gave him, he would have been far better off quietly sipping Guinness in the pub all alone, free from the decade he spent wasting away in her black widow's web.

For his own sanity and survival, Henry kept busy and stayed out of the house, especially on the weekends—stacking his Chrysler van with boxed sets of baseball cards, football jerseys, kitchen gadgets, books, bobble-head dolls, and just about every other type of sports memorabilia and heading to a flea market somewhere, usually on the South Shore. He'd set up his tables and line up his wares and goods in hopes of making a few dollars, then end up cramming most of it back into the van. It wasn't really about the money as much as it was something he enjoyed doing, as he had for years, along with other seniors like himself, most of them veterans, who traveled from flea market to flea market in places like Norwood or Walpole where they'd set up their tables in "their" spots.

Like most of his buddies, Henry bought and hoarded more stuff to sell than he actually sold. He had no bookkeeping method, and he kept all of his merchandise in the basement on Sanford Street. It was jammed down there, from floor to ceiling, with only small little walkways in between. Every square inch was accounted for, and over time, the stacks and piles fell over on one another, creating jumbled heaps, creating an impressive fire hazard, and making it impossible for him to know what he had down there with any accuracy.

When Henry went out, he never told my mother exactly where he was going, when he'd return, or how much he'd made. All of this infuriated her, and she was certain to share this at length with anyone and everyone. It was yet another useful example for her to use, yet another awful thing that Henry was "doing" to her that she could carry on about.

When Henry passed away, Ma saw dollar signs in the massive piles of "treasure" he'd left behind in the basement. She spent many an hour down there, rubbing her hands together and cackling at the thought of turning all of that junk into the world's biggest wad of sneakies. Between the house, his small life insurance policy, his veteran's surviving spouse pension she'd now receive, and the larder in the basement—modest as all that was—Henry left Ma more well-off than she could ever have dreamed, all without really having worked for anything a day in her life or contributed even one dollar to any household, in keeping with her blithe existence of always being taken care of.

I took care of all the paperwork, and once the life insurance was paid out and the pension checks starting coming in, Ma turned her attention in earnest to pressing us to turn what was no more than mountains of junk in the basement into cold hard cash. All we could do at first was stand paralyzed before the enormity of it and shake our heads, not knowing where to begin. Finally, Jody, Karen, Susan, and I made a plan to at least organize and catalog the entire lot to see what was there. Then we'd strategize how to try to sell it in bulk to some other junk-collecting flea-marketers to get the place cleaned out and Ma's bank account padded best we could. Most of the stuff was dated and not worth much, but it was mostly in good shape, although dry rot and mold had ruined a fair amount.

As we worked sorting through boxing and labeling things, Ma would come down to the basement periodically and hover like a sweatshop supervisor, making sure we didn't toss anything into the trash that she thought was sellable until we ran her off. Every once in a while she'd say half-heartedly, "You kids can take whatever you want, you know. I don't mind." Of course, she was hoping for the response of "no thanks, Ma" that we always gave. We each had enough crap in our own houses without adding any more of hers.

We were in the basement working one day, with Ma upstairs, when Susan unearthed a box at the bottom of a tall smelly pile of Red Sox and

Bruins sweatshirts. She discovered that it was full of dry rot and little piles of mouse droppings.

"Yuk, that's gross!" Susan cried as she stepped back, quickly dropping a soiled and moldy sweatshirt back onto the pile. "This whole box has *got to* go!" she said.

As we were all checking it out, we heard clomping on the stairs, and without warning the door to the basement was literally kicked open like a swinging saloon door in an old Western movie. There was Ma, in her scraggly robe and slippers, standing in the doorway looking ready for a gunfight.

"I heard what you said!" Ma said, accusing no one in particular.

"What are you talking about, Ma?" I said, laughing. She looked comical.

"Throw *what* out?" she demanded.

Although she liked to feign being hard of hearing, when it suited her, Ma could miraculously pick up a whisper between walls and certainly hear a shriek like Susan's coming from between the floorboards.

"Look at this shit, Ma," Susan showed her, holding out one of the rotting sweatshirts using an old curtain rod. "They're all like this!"

"Are you sure?" Ma asked, hope in her voice. "Can't we wash them or something?"

I just rolled my eyes and looked over at Jody, who was doing the same and shaking her head.

"Ma," I told her, "it's crap, and it's going out to the curb. No one would buy it like that!" I said in my firm, fatherly tone.

"Okay," she said, sounding meek now. "Whatever you think is best."

"Just go back upstairs, Ma, and let us keep working, okay?" Karen said. "We're busting our ass to clean all this shit out for you!"

Ma sighed, turned around, and went back upstairs, holding tight onto the rail and moving in slow motion, as if laboring, ignoring the fact that she'd come springing down the stairs as spry as a teenager just a moment before.

For almost two months of weekends, we worked on that basement, boxing and selling the stuff to flea marketers who advertised in the local papers or online. We picked up twenty dollars here, fifty dollars there, until finally it was all gone. Ma made about two thousand dollars all told, but that just made her sad and disappointed. Forget all the work we had done to clean up, package up, and sell a basement full of junk for her—all she could do was tell everyone how she knew we must have stolen from her, because there was no way she didn't get more money for *all that good stuff.* We didn't care that she criticized us as long as we knew we'd done the best we could for her, and at last we could put that dirty job behind us.

Now, as for David, between the way Ma treated him as her tormentor after Dad died and the way Ma's life with poor Henry was like watching a replay of his own childhood and our life with Dad, it became crystal clear to him that no matter what Dad may have done or not done, it was really Ma who had placed the firmest wedge between him and our father, negating any chance for them to have had any real relationship, if that were ever possible.

Like the rest of us, he'd bought completely into everything Ma said about Dad, and he'd spent his entire life in protective mode for her, all the while being hurt and angry at Dad without questioning anything. It now seemed like this was just a part of the elaborate hoax she'd played on all of us, and this part was especially painful for Dave, because he had already softened on his feelings for Dad over the years since the man had died out of some sense of forgiveness and regret, I suppose. The realization now, so many years later, that she was the main reason he never really knew his own father hurt him even more.

Still, in spite of that, once Henry was gone and Ma turned right back to him with renewed neediness, calling him day and night in her helpless voice and pleading with him to help with this or that or telling him how lonely she was, David, being who he was, came back to help. He did as much as he could stand to do before that final and full check-out left just me, Diane, and Susan to deal with her as best we were willing.

We chose our respective roles for our respective reasons. Diane continued on as primary errand girl, duty-bound through a lifetime of guilt and performing as Ma's surrogate and now further bound to her as a primary source of cigarettes and gas money. Susan, in her role as part-time caretaker, having harbored perhaps the least amount of overall resentment toward Ma since she was only five years old when Dad passed away, came by and cooked meals or cleaned up a little in the quiet hope that all her brother and sisters would somehow become closer than the scattered bunch we were.

And then there was me, in my designated position as Mighty Mike, acting now in the role of Ma's father figure, paying the bills, doling out her allowance, setting boundaries, and scolding her whenever she misbehaved.

I did so out of what I suppose was an inexplicable sense of obligation to the Fourth Commandment that the sisters had drilled into us so long ago on Mission Hill: *Honor thy mother and thy father.* And of course, there was my promise to Dad.

∽

Looking at Ma now, I wondered just who was that person living in there deep down inside of her and if I really ever knew who that real person was at all. I searched my memory for a time when we might have been emotionally close. When was that? It seemed like a stupid question, but it was an honest one. I knew she had to have been the one who kept me warm and fed and comforted as a crying infant, the one who warmed my baby bottles and rocked me to sleep in the middle of the night as those teeth that would eventually rot pushed their way through my gums. There are pictures of her holding me as a chubby baby, smiling and looking "normal." But looking at her now, it felt as though she couldn't have been the one who'd done any of that nurturing.

In college, I'd learned all about the British psychiatrist John Bowlby and his well-known theory of types of parental attachment and their impact on the development of our ability to move successfully through relationships and all of life's stages, so surely we'd had to have been bonded securely enough for me to turn out at least as semifunctional as I believed myself to be, right? His theories related how "emotionally positive" parents interacted with their children, starting at birth, to the level of lifelong security or insecurity that would likely result. I may have gotten off to a rocky start, but now I wasn't doing so bad, I figured, in spite of any exposure to her "emotionally negative" example.

An image of Ma cooling me with a sponge bath popped into my head. She had a concerned expression on her face. I was standing in my underwear on a toilet seat next to a sink. It was from the time when I was in second grade; we were living on the first floor of a triple-decker on Lamartine Street in Jamaica Plain. I'd been home from school and in and out of delirium from a stubborn fever for days.

Then I saw another scene from another apartment somewhere back in my jumbled history. She and Dad were waking us all up on a Christmas Eve for an unexpected treat of hot cocoa and Hershey bars. We split them into little squares and dropped them right into the steaming mugs, creating the most delicious chocolate concoction I'd ever tasted. We were watching the Charlie Brown Christmas special and sitting on the floor in the dark as a rotating light with a multicolored wheel whirled round and round, humming and magically reflecting first red, then green, then blue around the room, gleaming and glistening off of the artificial silver tree, all of this making even more exciting the promise of Christmas morning in all of our heads.

Where had that woman gone, and when had she been replaced by the seeming stranger who sat across from me now? Paul McCartney wrote "Let It Be" as an homage to his own mother, Mary, who died when he was only seventeen. Right up until her death, she had given him a lifetime full of hope, comfort, and inspiration. He was so moved by a mother's love that he gave the world a melody in which all could take comfort. For me, it only served as a reminder of how far from normal our relationship with Ma had been growing up and how none of us could turn to her in times of trouble, since it was she who was always the one in need.

I think to be fair to Ma, she did manage to take care of our basic needs when we were all very young—not yet of the age when our emotions and intelligence started to bloom and we needed wisdom or guidance to learn how to cope with even everyday things. We needed help to be secure enough in life to conquer fears and learn independence—to learn life lessons. At that juncture, I believe, she just didn't have any idea of what more to do beyond provide the bottles and the baths, other than to transfer to us all that she herself had become for lack of any other example or experience of her own.

If I had somehow made it to at least as far as I had now in spite of all that my parents did or didn't do, why had it been so different for my siblings? Of course there is always that nature versus nurture thing. Maybe it also had something to do with a theory by another psychologist, Rene Spitz, that I'd learned about. She suggested that life outcomes for some children of dysfunctional parents were dramatically affected by what she called the "psychotoxic" results of traumatic or inappropriate experiences to which they were exposed by those parents. Maybe things like those bathroom talks Ma had with my sisters impacted them, or her failure to provide protection from Dad's threats affected their subsequent feelings and attitude toward her now and their lives in general. As always, it was a combination of things. Among them, I guess, was the fact that there just wasn't a strong enough dose of good stuff from our parents, or others, injected into them throughout their individual childhoods to innoculate them against all the bad stuff.

It was easy enough for me to stand back and psychoanalyze the complete history of each of our lives growing up in a home like ours, with parents like ours, and to theorize why everyone felt the way that each did now. But the truth was, I could really only ever know my own personal experiences and how what I saw and heard and felt affected me. I'd gotten out early and away for good by eighteen, so I was blind to many of the impactful things the others had experienced.

Once I was gone off to the air force, beyond the occasional letter or phone call from one of my parents begging for money or seeking a call to action by Mighty Mike, I didn't have any day-to-day dealings with the family turmoil still going on back in Boston. This was much different from my brothers and sisters who, each in his or her own way, dealt for years with the craziness while working on personal physical and psychological exit strategies. A complete escape for many of them never became a reality.

Ma cleared her throat now and repeated her matter-of-fact report on how cigarettes and coffee had killed my father. She reached over and grabbed her own cigarette case, undid the clasp, removed a cigarette, and proceeded to light up. I was about to say something sarcastic, but I just let it go with a grin. She was eighty-one years old. Like every other part of her life, everything was well beyond changing.

"I'm almost out of butts," Ma said. "So good thing you brought me my shopping today."

"Well, they cost you almost $150 for the two cartons, Ma," I said. "Just imagine how much you could save in a year."

It wasn't an outright poke at her to tell her she ought to quit, but since hoarding money was her number-one love, followed by diabetic test strips, cigarettes, and pulp-free orange juice, in that order, I couldn't resist. She'd never lost the joy in her practice of keeping a stash of sneakies around the house, although there wasn't anyone left anymore from whom she needed to hide it. No matter; she'd take the money I'd give her each visit and stuff it into her cigarette case with the rest of the wad she already had stashed there and snap it tight in anticipation of counting it all once I left. Whenever I asked her how much money she had, she'd repeat that old refrain that she was broke.

"Speaking of money, did you bring me some?" Ma asked hopefully.

I hadn't passed over this visit's allowance yet, and she wanted to make sure I didn't leave without greasing her palm, as always.

"How much money do you have left, Ma?" I asked, being casual.

"Oh, not much, not much. I'm just about broke," she replied as expected. "I had to give Diane money for gas and to get me juice, and Eddie needed to borrow forty dollars so he could get some food, but he always pays me back! He's a good boy."

Eddie borrowed from Ma a couple of times a month, with Diane acting as the go-between, so that he could sustain his diet of Dunkin' Donuts coffee, submarine sandwiches, and Hostess chocolate cupcakes. It was true that he did pay her back every time from his Social Security disability check when it came in each first of the month.

I knew she had to have at least a few hundred dollars in her clutches, but I just wanted to hear her tell me she was broke so I could tell Jody later that she was true to form again today and share a laugh. Ma was still within budget, so I reached into my pocket for the folded wad of bills and handed her the usual $150 allowance, all in twenties, tens, and fives so it would seem like more to her. She reached out, catlike, and pulled it in with her nicotine-stained fingers as her eyes darted around, as though she were being watched. She whispered, "Thank you," and our clandestine deal was done.

I knew as soon as I left, she'd take out the rest of her sneakies and, with great care, count her stash and ensure it was placed in denominational order. She would then calculate how many diabetic test strips or cartons of orange juice it would get her in a pinch.

"You're welcome, Ma. And you have to make that last till next time, okay?" I said as I always did after lining her pockets.

"Do you think maybe I should keep at least one blank check here, you know, in case of an emergency or something?" she asked.

She'd try this every once in a while, and I did feel a little bad keeping her checkbook from her, but there'd been too many bounced checks and fees, so it was for her own protection. She'd sent Diane out to turn a check into cash to add to her countinghouse too many times, and never for an emergency. When I asked her why she just didn't use the money she already had, she'd say she "forgot" she had money and that she wasn't getting any younger and her memory wasn't always perfect, didn't I know? She was careful not to act too addled too often, as she knew this would lead to us talking about maybe it was time for her to consider other living arrangements, so she picked her spots with care.

"Ma, you know one of us always takes care of any emergencies for you, like the time the water heater went, right?"

She couldn't so much as take out the trash, let alone deal with a busted pipe or something.

"That's why I have power of attorney too, remember?" I continued. "That way I can help you even when I'm not right here, so don't worry about emergencies, okay?"

"You do a good job," she said. "I trust you with everything, you know that. You were always a good boy. I remember the time you won that award in fourth grade for being a polite citizen."

It was surprising that she remembered that, yet alone brought it up. "It was a citizenship award, Ma," I said. "Yeah, I remember. I got it when I was in the fourth grade at the Philbrick School in Roslindale."

We were living then on Hyde Park Avenue on the Roslindale-Hyde Park line on the second floor of yet another triple-decker, right next to the parking lot from the long-gone Massimino's Italian restaurant with its wonderful aroma, although we never ate there. The big blue slate-shingled house sat up elevated from the street, with a six foot wall in the front where we'd hang out on summer nights. The apartment was big and drafty, with large gabled windows in the living room that faced the street and jutted out so far you could look out to the right down Hyde Park Avenue almost a mile toward Forest Hills and to the left just as far toward Cleary Square.

I loved kneeling on the floor with my elbows on the ample windowsills with the lights out at night, looking down on the bustling street scene with the neon lights flashing from Macy's liquor mart and the dry cleaner's and convenience store across the street where I bought my Green Lantern and horror comic books. I marveled at the steady stream of gleaming headlights that came toward the house from both directions, and I squinted my eyes almost all the way shut to make the beams look as though hundreds of stars were shining directly at me, only me.

I must have been going through some strange latent separation anxiety stage when we lived there, because I found myself, for some unknown reason, getting nervous and worried about my parents whenever they left the house after dark to run errands or go on a visit to a relative's house—maybe to pick up a borrowed twenty dollar bill or some donated food. My imagination would run away from me, and I'd fear something horrible had happened to them and that they'd never be coming back.

Maybe there was a horrific car accident, or somebody robbed and hurt them out there in the night, or maybe they just weren't coming back because they didn't want us anymore. What would happen to us then? My parents had always threatened that if we didn't behave, they would ship us off to the Home for Little Wanderers, an orphanage in Jamaica Plan just opposite the Veteran's Affairs hospital, so I wondered if perhaps that's where we'd be taken and what kind of food they would have.

I'd kneel there in the dark, hunkered in the windowsill imagining those ridiculous things and straining my eyes to see Dad's Rambler wagon pull up next to the curb like it inevitably did whenever they went out. I was fine if they left and returned in the daylight, but once it got dark, the dread would come over me. Although they always returned, that didn't prevent my anxiety from recurring every time they were out after dark until they made it home again.

"Oh, yes, that's right. It was a special award for being the politest boy in the whole school!" she said.

It was toward the end of the school year, and my fourth-grade teacher, Mrs. McMillan, had asked me to stay after class, where she handed me a sealed envelope that had my mother's name handwritten on it in Mrs. McMillan's flowing penmanship.

"Now you take this straight home and give it to your mother, okay?" instructed Mrs. McMillan. "And don't you open it," she added.

I couldn't imagine anything I'd done wrong to deserve a note home to my parents, but I only said, "Yes, Mrs. McMillan." I walked, somber, over the two blocks back to the apartment, full of wonder and dread at what could be in that envelope and confused that I couldn't figure it out. Ma was in the kitchen drinking tea at the table and smoking a cigarette. WRKO was on the radio, and Peter, Paul, and Mary were singing "Puff the Magic Dragon."

I handed Ma the mysterious envelope and just stood there waiting for whatever shoe was about to fall. Ma tore it open, read it, smiled, and then put it on the table before bending down to give me a quick hug.

"You're the best boy in the whole school!" she exclaimed.

I could only manage a soft, "What?"

"It says right here: 'Michael David Boudreau has been selected as the citizenship award recipient for the John D. Philbrick Elementary School for school year 1966, signed, James R. Lernigan, principal'!"

I wasn't sure what had made me such a good citizen, but the letter said I was one. Might it have been because I played George Washington in the fourth-grade play and didn't forget even one line? Or maybe it was my guitar solo during the school's talent show, where I stood on stage and misplayed the two repetitive chords from the theme to *Peter Gunn*, a popular detective show back in the sixties, over and over and almost inaudibly for about five minutes until the teacher cleared her throat indicating that perhaps I needed to wrap it up? All I could do was stumble between the two chords, and once I started alternating between them, I didn't know which one to end with, so I was very grateful for her signal.

Ma was beaming with pride about the letter from school, and she couldn't wait to tell my father all about it as soon as he got home from work. I was surprised when he told me how proud of me he was. I got to stay up late on a school night to watch the Red Sox on television while the others had to go to bed, making me feel a bit but not completely guilty about my sudden celebrity status

"And do you remember Dad bought you a bike for winning?" Ma was now saying.

"Wow, I'd forgotten about that," I said, although I hadn't. It was a couple of nights later, and my parents had gone out. I found myself once again staring out of the living room window in the dark, straining for any sign of their return. They were later than usual this time, and my heart was racing with a growing fear that this was going to be the night they really wouldn't be coming back. When they finally pulled up, I raced out to the kitchen and back to my abandoned homework, pretending I'd been doing it all along. Now I was able to concentrate, and my anxiety was starting to slip away.

Ma came through the apartment front door, passed through the living room, and then walked down the hall to the kitchen. "Hey you," she said, in a cheerier-than-usual voice. "Your father needs you downstairs to help him carry something."

All I could think was maybe he'd hit his numbers again and was bringing Ma home a new television or something for their bedroom. I pushed away from my geography homework and ran down the two flights of stairs to the front of the house, where my father was waiting on the porch, grinning about something.

"Whaddya think, pal?" Dad asked, pleased with himself. Still in his work clothes, he was steadying a shiny new Columbia Flyer bicycle by the handlebars as my eyes swept over it in disbelief.

"Is that for me?" I said in hopeful expectation, afraid to get excited and wondering what in the world was happening and why. Was it the citizenship award? It must be!

"Yup, ain't it a fuckin beauty? Take it for a spin!" Dad said, carrying it down to the sidewalk. It was a beauty all right. It was candy-apple red with white pinstripes, and it had huge chrome fenders that reflected the brilliant light shining down from the streetlamp. The handlebars were just as shiny, with long red and white tassels streaming down from the white rubber grips. It really was a new bike, and it really was mine.

I jumped up onto the seat that was a little too high, but I managed to pedal with the balls of my feet as my thumbs worked the bell and gearshift mounted on either side of the handlebars. I raced up and down the sidewalk before squeezing the brake grips a little too hard. The tires screeched as I slid to a stop in front of Dad.

"Easy," he said. "You'll wear out the brakes if you do that too much."

"Right," I said, a little out of breath but feeling on top of the world. I'd never seen or touched anything so new and perfect, and it was mine!

"Here," Dad said, handing me a padlock and chain. "Keep it in the basement locked to the pole." He turned and went upstairs.

I stood there for another minute or so admiring the bike in disbelief, and then I walked it up the driveway, careful to avoid potholes, and then back around to the bulkhead at the back of the house. I unhinged the kickstand and carefully propped the bike up while I opened the heavy bulkhead doors to expose the few steps leading down to the basement. I negotiated the stairs one at a time, then ducked down so as not to bang my head at the bottom of the steps. I was more careful not to bang up the bike.

I chained the bike up as Dad had told me, being extra cautious not to scratch the paint, and as I stood there giving it one last long look, I felt suddenly sad. None of my brothers and sisters had ever been given a bike. It was one thing to let me stay up late for a night to watch the Red Sox, but this was something altogether different.

But wait a minute. I'd won an award for being a very good citizen, hadn't I? Maybe if *they* were nicer or were in the talent contest at school, they'd have won an award and gotten a present too, right? Why should I feel bad? I deserved it, didn't I?

But even as I rationalized, all I could think about was how the others would feel. They'd pretend they didn't care, but I knew they'd be hurt. Right then and there, I made up my mind that it would belong to all of us, no matter how much it made me wince to think of them scratching it up because they'd never take care of it like I would. But that would be okay.

Looking back, I suppose getting a gleaming bike that night *did* give me a story that was just about me—one story I could have shared with my air force buddies on Father's Day about one special night when I think my father really was proud of me and how it made me feel, for the first time, that I was important to him. Important enough for him to spend money I knew we didn't have on a shiny new bike. Assuming he bought it.

"Oh, yeah," I said to Ma. "Now I remember. Wasn't it a red bike or something?"

"Yes, exactly," Ma said. "It was a big red bike for being a polite citizen!"

"It was a citizenship award, Ma," I repeated, rolling my eyes, but she wasn't listening anymore. She reached over to the coffee table and picked up what looked like an old brown letter or certificate of some kind that was stored inside one of those shiny document protectors that were usually kept in a three-ring binder.

"Oh, I thought you might want this," she said, handing it over and then leaning back in her recliner, looking as proud as if she'd made it herself.

What is this? I thought. Had she really kept the letter from Mrs. McMillan all these years?

CHAPTER 11

I'm what you call a deathbed Catholic.

—BRODERICK CRAWFORD

I took the plastic sleeve and scanned the old document. The paper was badly yellowed, almost brown, and it looked more than a little fragile. The typing was faded in most areas but darker in some, and it was specked with strike-overs and full of spacing errors and typos. Across the top of the brittle paper, in capital letters, were the words, "UNITED STATES COAST GUARD." It was dated 3 May 1946, and it had my father's name on it along with his service serial number 685-419 typed below the subject line of the letter, which read, "Information for your guidance subsequent to discharge."

"I thought you might want it," Ma said. "Since you were in the service too, like your father. I found it in that plastic tub with all the old pictures in the back bedroom."

Over the years since Dad had died, I'd realized more and more just how little I knew about him and his past—nothing, when it came right down to it, about who he was, what he experienced, what daily life had been like for him, or what moved him. I knew and remembered him in only one dimension, because all any of us ever saw was his outward persona. His was our tyrannical father, nothing more. I couldn't even guess at what his deepest and most passionate feelings might have been about, or what it was that might have meant the most to him.

What were his dreams? What went through his mind on those nights when he'd sit alone in the living room, gently rocking in the recliner, his cigarette glowing in the dark, apparently lost deep in his own thoughts as

Frank Sinatra crooned "My Way" in the background? Surely they couldn't all have been purely sexual.

What was his childhood like? What about living life as a skinny teenager, just as I had? What were his deep regrets? Did he even have any? Most of us do, right? God knows he had plenty to ponder. Did he think about his first wife and wonder about the son he never mentioned and who none of us learned about until years later? He never shared even one inner revelation to me, even as he lay dying, even as he must have been taking some stock of his life.

What about our family history? What about his father and his grandfather, two men I never knew and whose names were never even mentioned? There was never any sense of legacy passed on to us by our parents from either side of the family, really—no stories of some great-great-grandfather who maybe came over from somewhere in France or served in the French and Indian War, or of a grand matriarch on either side of the family who perhaps opened the first school in a small village in Maine and was famous throughout the county for her blueberry pies. I did have a couple of old black-and-white photographs of my mother's grandparents taken in the 1920s in Maine, but I knew nothing about them other than what someone had written in pencil on the back of each photo.

On the back of the picture of my great-grandmother was written, "Emma Diane Morin, born June 30, 1876 in Riviere-du-Loupe, Quebec, Canada, died Aug 28, 1952." The photo showed a woman with a stern gaze looking with my mother's eyes right into the camera. She was leaning in a doorway wearing a starched white apron, her hair tied up in a tight bun almost straight up on top of her head.

Looking at my great-great-grandfather's photo, I could see a close resemblance to my mother's brothers around the eyes and cheekbones. He had a shaggy beard and was wearing farmer jeans and a straw hat but had an expression on his face that was a bit softer than his wife's. On the back of that photo was written, "Felix Joseph Nadeau, born Feb 22, 1870 in Riviere-du-Loupe, Quebec, Canada, died Jun 29, 1969."

Until I saw those pictures, I'd assumed both great-grandfathers had died long before I was born, since no one in the family ever mentioned either of them. Those photos always urged me to do more research and find out more on my own about both sides of the family. As for my parents, their own legacy is for others to define as they will.

Beyond just knowing that he'd been in the Coast Guard, I had no other details about Dad's time in the military until my mother handed me this faded letter, an actual artifact from my father's history that at least told me something new. It was issued to my father by the Coast Guard Civil Readjustment Office, Separation Center #1, located at the still existing Boston Coast Guard Station, and signed by a Lieutenant JG Helen Reich. It served to advise my father on the rules of returning to civilian life in terms of things like wearing the uniform and the requirement to report to the draft board, and on the back it listed a host of addresses of agencies ranging from the Veterans Administration to the unemployment office to help him in his transition to the civilian workforce. My father's immature signature was at the bottom in faded pencil where he acknowledged receipt, thereby ending his obligation to the Coast Guard.

Doing the math based upon the date of the letter, he would have been nineteen years old at the time of his discharge in 1946. I knew he'd never finished high school, so one of his parents must have signed him into the service when he was only seventeen. It must have been for a two-year hitch, as the minimum age to enlist was otherwise eighteen. Having started my military career at eighteen years old myself, I felt that his having the courage to sign into the military at such a young age didn't fit with the man I saw growing up—the man who hid from other men behind rolled-up car windows and seemed to be a threat only to women and children. He'd been somehow successful in completing boot camp and surviving for at least two years in a macho forties-era military full of tough men, many of whom were serving time in the service as a court-presented alternative to time in jail.

I'd never tracked down his discharge papers to see if it was under conditions less than honorable, as that would reveal the actual terms of his enlistment and tell whether or not his original hitch was supposed to be longer or if he got discharged earlier for any number of causes, such as unfit for service or disciplinary reasons. I wasn't sure I wanted to know. Either way, I had to commend him for giving it a go for his country in wartime, so I considered his discharge to be honorable. Still, I wondered how he had handled it all.

I remembered how homesick I had felt, especially those first few nights in Texas when I was going through boot camp. I'd lie wide awake in the middle of the night with everything quiet other than the cacophony of snores echoing through the stifling open-bay barracks that housed me and my fellow recruits. Back then, I was still very anxious about my mother's well-being back home, and of course I missed my girlfriend. *Why didn't I just go to college,* I'd think in regret, *even if it was only to a state school?* My imagination would run wild about what could be happening back home, and I'd often stifle sobs in the dark, feeling the isolation.

I heard some of the other guys doing the same, and I was sure they were feeling just as insecure and homesick. As dawn approached, my apprehension would build at knowing the inevitable roar of the drill instructor would come barging in at precisely five in the morning to roust fifty young men in T-shirts and tighty-whiteys from their perfectly aligned rows of bunks into an organized frenzy of quick showers and shaves, and another day of marching and shouting in the Texas heat. In spite of all that, deep down I knew I really wanted to be there and to stick it out and prove something to myself.

I could only imagine how Dad might have felt some nights when he found himself wedged in the tiny crawlspace of a bunk that he'd share in shifts with the other sailors on his ship as it cruised across some coastal waters somewhere, lights blinking in the dark and reflecting off the waves. I pictured him lying there, hands clasped behind his head as the boat pitched to and fro, probably fearful but excited about the adventures in the unknown that lay ahead, but perhaps lonely too, because like me, he'd never before put himself into a place where at the end of the day, he really only had himself to rely on

For me, that being alone at the end of the day—starting on that first night in basic training and so far from home in Boston—was the true beginning of my breaking away from the emotional cobwebs I'd been living in. For the first time, my focus was truly on myself, on the here and now, with immediate goals, objectives, and challenges to be met that were centered strictly on me. It felt okay. I started to learn what it meant to measure success one day at a time, and for the first time, I realized the possibility for a new life far beyond a childhood dominated by overstuffed cardboard boxes, cockroaches, and abscessed teeth.

Those same thoughts of our shared fledgling beginning in the military, although decades apart, occurred to me on the day I came back from Germany in 1980 and walked into the dark living room in Roslindale to see a shell of a man I was supposed to believe was my father, sitting alone and smoking a cigarette in pajamas and a flimsy robe, suffering with the ravages of the disease I would watch eat him to death, mercilessly, hour by hour, day by day, for the next six months.

While home on that visit, I applied for and was granted what the air force calls a "humanitarian reassignment" back to Hanscom Air Force

Base in Bedford, Massachusetts, in keeping with their policy of temporarily moving military members back to the base nearest their hometown in the event an immediate family member becomes terminally ill. By the end of October, I was cleared out of Germany and living in the barracks at Hanscom, and I began my ritual of heading into Roslindale pretty much every day after work to spend time with him and help out in any other way I could. I'd go in every Saturday too, but I reserved most Sundays for myself to recharge my physical and emotional batteries.

For the most part, Dad stuck close to his bed. He spent his days lying there smoking and watching game shows and candlepin bowling—the closest thing to a sport he ever really enjoyed doing. For years, he'd been in work leagues that bowled out of the old Empire Lanes on River Street in Hyde Park, and the annual bowling banquet was the social event of the year for him and my mother. It was held at venues such as the VFW or American Legion Post with the rusting tank out front in Dedham, and it would be the one time of the year my father might get a little tipsy after two or three Budweisers, although he didn't drink very often otherwise. Cigarettes, coffee, porn magazines, and dime-store detective novels with the covers torn off were his vices.

"Thanks, Ma," I said now after looking over the document. "This is pretty cool. I'll have to show David. He'll get a kick out of it too."

"I think there's a couple more pictures of your father in his uniform stuck in that box too, if you want to try to find them," Ma offered. "I don't want them," she said almost offhandedly.

"Sure, thanks. I'll go through the box next time I'm down," I replied.

"Oh, I almost forgot," Ma said. "Look what else I have for you!" She reached down beside her chair, grabbed a plastic shopping bag, and held it out to me with her yellow grin.

I took the bag and was at once overcome by the stench of nicotine. Holding it with both hands, I could feel a familiar thick triangular object wrapped inside the oversized and tacky plastic bag. After unfolding the sticky wrapping, I reached in and pulled out an American flag and saw that the heavy canvas cloth, although now yellowed and stained, was still folded as tight and perfect as it was on the day of my father's funeral over thirty years before.

It had been draped over his coffin, signifying that he'd been a veteran, and then folded the right way by someone following the service and presented to my mother to keep. I had folded many such flags during my time in the honor guard while in the air force, although not always on such somber occasions; more often when someone retired, although I did my fair share of funeral details and presented the flag to a grieving widow "on the behalf of a grateful nation."

Dad's should have been encased in a glass-covered shadow box or something to preserve and honor it, but it had been thoughtlessly stuffed into a plastic bag and shoved on a shelf, it seemed, wherever my mother moved to after Dad died. In its deteriorated condition, I knew I'd have to take it to the base to be burned with honor as is the proper ceremonial disposition of worn or damaged American flags. I wondered now why I hadn't placed it in a case myself for her all those years ago.

"Thanks for this too, Ma," I said. "I'll take good care of it."

"I brought him some red, white, and blue flowers in a vase with a small flag sticking out of them for his room at the Deaconess right before he died, remember?" she said quietly. There was almost pride in her voice, but suddenly her lip started to tremble a little, and out of nowhere, tears began to fill her eyes. Somehow, this particular memory had caught her off guard.

"It's okay, Ma," I said softly. It caught me off guard as well to see her so quickly brought to tears over that memory—any memory. Her remembering that detail about the vase surprised me, and I didn't want to upset her any more by pointing out that by then, Dad was in a morphine-induced stupor, as he was close to the end, and he likely didn't even know the vase was there, let alone that he had visitors.

Those last weeks with him in the hospital were for me a blur of rides back and forth from the base in Bedford to the New England Deaconess Hospital, just off of the Fenway in Boston. It was in a clustered complex of dozens of clinics and other hospitals that ran up and down Longwood Avenue, stretching almost all the way to Kenmore Square.

We took turns making sure someone was there every day or night to visit him and report back to everyone on how he was doing, as if sharing an unspoken and morbid deathwatch. There was very little emotion displayed by anyone as we performed this automatic duty. It was as though we were more like curious bystanders, looking on awkwardly, anticipating the inevitable, knowing they should feel something but not really sure just what that should be.

Even my mother seemed in control and out of character, forsaking a prime opportunity to solicit further pity and attention and make my father's dying all about her. I couldn't recall once seeing her hold his hand or say a comforting word while he was in the hospital; nor did anyone else, I suppose, for that matter, as far as I knew. Even in his last days, our biggest worry still, as always, was "how Ma was doing," although along with the emotional numbness, we all felt some sense of impending liberation for her. It was only later, of course, that we would come to realize that she was really never a captive to all of her "suffering and abuse" at the hands of Georgie; more like a volunteer for the job.

It was a raw and rainy Saturday morning in April when he died. My mother was on her way back to the hospital with Judy after having gone home for a bit to get some rest. Diane and Loretta were down the hall in the waiting room, grabbing a cup of coffee and taking a break from the stifling air in my father's room. He had just been brought back up to his room on a gurney from the ICU where he'd spent the last two days. It was placed parallel to the hospital bed, and I was standing at the foot of it listening to his raspy and rattling breathing in between the beeps of the heart monitor and waiting for the nurses to come back in and lift him back into his bed and for the priest to arrive. I'd called Father Patrick at the hospital staff's urging and my own sense that Dad was fading fast.

His right hand was lying on his chest, his fingers making a slightly clenched fist around a cluster of holy medals that were tangled around a crucifix. I was struggling to figure out why I wasn't feeling what I thought I should be feeling—whatever the hell that was. Where was the sadness? That sense of profound loss one should feel as a parent's life was slipping away before your eyes? Death was starting to show itself to me in my father's face, and I was feeling empty and blank. I had stood in the shower for over an hour one night just days before trying to force myself to conjure up something definitive about my feelings, some imagery of what my emotional reaction to my own father's death would be, should be, but I got only a white screen.

I kept asking myself, "Why can't I *feel* something, dammit? Where are the tears?" All I heard was the echoing sound of silence coming from the deepest part of my soul. Whatever I imagined I was trying to see down there—and there was definitely something—was hiding as silent as a stone, deep in the shadows, stubborn and unwilling to show itself, at least for now.

Looking at him lying there, not quite conscious, I wondered what last thoughts, if any, were going through his mind as he mumbled from time to time, too softly to hear, still clutching the medals as the morphine drip did its job. Occasionally, his eyes would fly wide open, and he'd look right at me with recognition for a few whole seconds or so with what seemed like a pleading expression and move his mouth as if trying to say something, though it was difficult to know. I let myself imagine he was trying to tell me he was sorry for something … everything. Somehow, the thought of a bedside confession terrified me and put a lump in my throat, and I felt my eyes getting a little moist. Oh, where was that priest?

I tried to push the thoughts away, but I still found myself thinking that if he was saying he was sorry for something, I would tell him that I was sorry too—sorry for that night back on Bradeen Street when my heart was so full of rage, sorry for telling him that I hated him that night. I was only a kid then, and I was mad, and I didn't know what else to do to hurt him beyond the shoves and the shouts and those piercing words meant to injure, because that's all I had as weapons. I was really angry too because all I ever wanted was for him to have seen me—really seen me; for him to have recognized my fears and showed me how to conquer them; for him to have taught me so much more than to always remember that it was better to "tuck it to them before they tucked it to you"; to have prepared me, at least a little bit, for what was out there in the world; to have been the kind of father to me that my friends all seemed to have had; to have told me even once how proud he was of me for making the hockey team and to have come to at least one of my games.

I wiped away the surprising wetness from my eyes with the palms of both hands, trying to fight my racing thoughts. I took a deep breath, my emotions catching me by surprise as they started to stir. *No, I won't feel this way now, not now*, I thought. I tried to block the sudden waves of memories, but they kept coming and coming.

They took me back to when I was twelve years old and so depressed and sad. I felt a million miles away from him, and so lying in bed one night, I started to cry out loud for him for reasons I still don't understand. I'd been lying there sobbing, as I often did during that time, hating myself and my life, and everything just came bubbling out of me almost uncontrollably. I hated that my teeth were rotten and I couldn't smile without placing a hand over my mouth, and I hated my spindly body and imagined my arms looked like toothpicks so I kept them covered, sometimes in layers of sweatshirts so I'd look bigger to the other boys.

All those feelings and thoughts overwhelmed me sometimes, so in bed that night I cried, as I often did—only this time, he had to have heard me, so for whatever reason, he came in. He sat at the edge of the bed as I turned away to face the wall, embarrassed at my tears and him having heard me and his being there at all. He rubbed the back of my neck, and I knew we both felt awkward. He told me he loved me and that he knew I was out there making great catches on the baseball field, and he said he'd get to one of my games sometime soon, don't you worry. It made me nauseous; it all seemed so hollow.

He tried to say something comforting, but it just came out stumbling and stilted. All I could think about was the bad stuff he'd done to Ma and everyone, and I hated myself even more for caring about him. I just wanted him to take his hand off of me and tell him to go away. As my sobbing subsided, I stared at the wall facing away from him, disgusted with myself for allowing him to think I needed him and despising him for letting things get to the way they had for us all and for making me wish that he wasn't my father.

He pulled away then, telling me to "Sleep tight, pal," and he went back to his room and whatever weirdness went on in there between him and Ma. It's the only time I can remember my father ever touching me other than hitting me or that awkward hug we gave each other in his living room when I came back from Germany to see him already half-dead in the dark. Watching him lying there now so still, I could feel death standing by mute and patient as a vulture, knowing the time was soon. I had to turn my eyes away, feeling guilty and horrible that the memory of that night he came to my room dared come to me now and that it could still fill me with disgust, even as he lay there with labored breathing, his broken body clinging to life between gasps for air.

How could I be thinking of myself, and why was I feeling angry at him at this moment? Why now? I hadn't thought about that ugliness in years.

Maybe those deep-down feelings that had been eluding me were guilty ones for still harboring a residual anger that found itself raging against his daring to die now, so young, with the dubious legacy of perpetrating a decades-long list of unresolved hurts and abuses, leaving behind a family that was mired in a hopeless tangle of perpetual dysfunction, with all of his children trying to find their own way in the world without a map.

I heard the door to Dad's room opening behind me and turned to see that it was, mercifully, Father Patrick. He walked over and stood next to me, placing a hand on my shoulder.

"How is he doing, Michael?" the priest asked with compassion in his voice, although he already knew the answer.

"Thanks for coming, Father. I'm not sure how aware he is of anything, but thank God, he's not in pain. I was hoping he'd be with us long enough to receive last rites. Can you do anything?" I asked, hopeful, but in the back of my mind wondering if God would even consider forgiveness for someone who, as far as I knew, only turned to God in his darkest hour, as so many souls do.

Father Patrick moved toward the head of the gurney and placed his hand on Dad's forehead gently. He motioned for me to move around to the other side, opposite of where he stood. Just as I did so, Dad's eyes opened, and he looked at Father Patrick, who had removed his hand and was returning Dad's gaze with a comforting smile. Dad's expression told me that he was aware that we were there, as he now turned his head toward me and moved his hand a little in my direction.

I reached down and held it. His skin felt like parchment. With as much grip as he could muster, I could feel him pulling me down toward him as his mouth started to move, but nothing came out but a rattling cough. I leaned in close to him as he cleared his throat best he could, straining to say something. I could see his life receding in his sunken eyes as they locked on to mine, and he lifted his head about an inch from the pillow. In no more than a hoarse whisper, he mouthed, "Take care of your mother for me" in a voice I didn't recognize. Then he let his head fall back onto the pillow, his blank eyes still open but looking straight ahead as he let out a deep exhale.

"Of course, Dad, I will," I promised, still holding his hand. *Hasn't it always been about taking care of Ma?* I couldn't help but think.

"George," Father Patrick said, "can you hear me?"

Dad let go of my hand and turned his head now toward Father Patrick, indicating he could, but he didn't speak.

Father Patrick looked at my father in earnest and said, "George, would you like me to administer the last rites of the Church to you?"

He was referring to one of the seven sacraments of the Catholic faith, called *extreme unction*. As is true for each of the sacraments, the sacrament of extreme unction is based in scripture. According to the traditional Roman Catholic teachings, the author of James 5:14–15 calls for priests to pray over the sick and to anoint them "in the name of the Lord." It is believed this sacred action has the power to save the ill and dying and to forgive sins, and if Dad was going to die, I wanted him to have any possible shot at somehow passing through heaven's gate, or at least getting to purgatory, even as I suppressed my doubts it would work for him. We'd just have to leave that to God.

I was worried, though, because I knew there were conditions required before Father Patrick could conduct the sacrament, and it didn't look as though Dad was in any shape to comply. The person who is ill or injured must have achieved the age of reason, seven years old, so he met that criteria. However, he must also repent of his sins and be in a state of grace, and to achieve that requires the ill or dying person to first recite a prayer, called the Act of Contrition, and then complete a repetition of baptismal promises or the recital of another prayer called the Apostles' Creed. That's followed by the priest reciting the Lord's Prayer and administering the Holy Eucharist. Only then can the priest perform the sacrament of extreme unction.

Looking at Dad fading fast, I didn't see how any of that was possible. "Father Patrick, I know he's clear-minded enough to want last rites now," I said, "but I don't think he's strong enough to do it. What do we do?" I heard sudden concern in my voice, while at the same time I was fighting the fleeting thought of *what's the use anyway?*

My father's breathing was becoming more labored and accompanied by a harsh, raspy gurgling coming from his throat. I could see he was straining to keep his eyes open, but they kept fluttering. He slowly moved his arm and placed his right hand over his heart and the cluster of tangled holy medals that were lying against his chest and tucked inside his pajama top. His gaunt appearance reminded me of the old haunting black-and-white photos of prisoners taken at concentration camps like the ones I'd seen in the museum when visiting Dachau, Germany.

Father Patrick looked at me with reassurance. "It's okay, Michael. The apostolic blessing with plenary indulgence at the hour of death should be imparted to those who desire it while still rational and conscious. I'd say your father responded in the affirmative when I asked him. Extreme unction may also be granted to anyone who has given any indication of such desire or has seemed contrite before becoming unconscious or irrational. He indicated his desire, but from what you know, has he seemed contrite for his sins? In my prior meetings with him, that indeed seemed to be the case. Would you agree?"

The truth was, I really didn't know. My father hadn't shared with me any such thoughts or feelings over the last few months as I sat with him night after night hovering over the cribbage board, watching television, or sharing cups of coffee. A few times, it seemed like he was trying to take the conversation somewhere that touched on the past. Perhaps he really did want to say something about his own deep personal thoughts or about our family. Regrets, maybe? But those were nothing more than endings of awkward conversations. They trailed off, and I never pressed him. But it did leave me wondering if he was actually struggling inside at all with reconciling what his life had been with what would soon become his afterlife. Surely there was sorrow and regret for what might have been better—for him, for everyone whose life he touched. Wouldn't we all take stock if we knew the end was near? Play back the film?

"Yes, I'd agree, Father," I said, needing to believe my own words for Dad's sake.

"Very good, then," Father Patrick replied, pulling a small vial of holy oil from his pocket. He began the sacrament with, "Let us begin by reciting the Lord's Prayer."

We did so aloud together. Then, dipping the vial, he wet his fingertips with the oil and began making the sign of the cross on various parts of Dad's body. After making the last sign on Dad's forehead, he said, "Through this Holy Unction or oil, and through the great goodness of His mercy, may God pardon thee whatever sins thou hast committed by evil use of sight, hearing, smell, taste, speech, touch, and ability to walk."

Again, I had to push thoughts out of my head—thoughts of the soul-tarnishing sins Dad may have committed in each of those categories. Eyes closed, Father Patrick made the sign of the cross, and I somberly did the same. I was not sure if I was supposed to do so as well.

"I'll leave you alone to spend some time now," Father Patrick said kindly.

"Thank you for everything, Father," I replied.

"You're most welcome. I'll see you soon," he said, I'm sure referring to the funeral parlor in Roslindale Square that we had standing by to receive my father.

"Take care, Michael," Father Patrick said with finality as he turned and left the room, leaving me to that blankness of feeling that had by now returned, insulating me from those racing and random thoughts of the moments before. I was only twenty-two, and I had encountered death just once before—when one of my high-school classmates, star of the football and basketball teams, had drowned in a tragedy at a house party celebrating the end of senior year. He hadn't even been drinking. It was surreal then, and all of us were sad but relieved in private that it hadn't happened to us or our families, reinforcing our young and preposterous notions of immortality. Death only happened to other people.

Looking at Dad now, I fully grasped that the brilliant light in each of us would be snuffed out with cold certainty, and I couldn't help but again allow myself to feel temporary and selfish relief at the fact that I was young and, God willing, I still had over fifty years left if I could at least make it to the average age of death for men. Still, I had to fight the thought that what was happening to Dad now *would* happen to me, one way or another.

Just then, David and two nurses from the floor came bursting into the room, startling me from that thought. Dave nodded in my direction, and then he came over and stood next to me. The first nurse was a short redhead who looked too young to me to be a nurse, but she moved with the purpose of a seasoned expert. The other nurse was in her fifties and very sturdy at what had to be over six feet tall. The two of them would have been a comical sight under different circumstances.

"We were just waiting for Father Patrick to finish his visit before coming in to move your father back into his bed," the younger of the two nurses explained with a smile. I nodded my understanding, and David and I stepped back to allow them to get into position at the head and foot off the gurney. I'm sure Dad weighed no more than eighty-something pounds at this point, so I knew they could easily move him. The taller of the two was gentle as she placed her arms under Dad's armpits and wrapped her hands around what was left of his shoulders, while the other wrapped her arms with care around his lower legs.

"Okay," said the older nurse. "Let's lift on three." The other nurse nodded.

"Here we go then: one, two, and three," said the tall nurse, and with perfect timing and economy of motion, they lifted my father up as they sidestepped, swinging him gently into position above the waiting bed. Everything seemed to be in slow motion as he hovered there, hanging limp in their arms. The stark image of his broken body reminded me of the *Pieta*, Michelangelo's beautiful sculpture that I'd seen in the Vatican in Rome that depicted Jesus dead and cradled in the loving arms of Mary.

As the nurses carefully lowered my father to the bed, he suddenly tensed up all over, and a deep, loud, rattling gurgle came rushing from his throat just as he came to rest on the bed. Then he was silent, head thrown back, eyes wide open. His right hand was still clutching the holy medals around his neck. The beeping from the heart monitor turned to a steady, insistent tone. The nurses seemed oddly calm as the taller of the two came around the bed to check his pulse. She looked with a compassionate expression toward us to tell us what we already knew. He had passed.

Dave and I stood there, motionless as Dad was, and I stared at Dad almost curiously, thinking that the body before me wasn't even him anymore but someone or something else, because once a soul leaves a body, what is there left really? Only those worldly things left behind for others to finish—to somehow deal with.

The nurses seemed to be waiting for one of us to say something. My father had just died right before my eyes, and all of my emotions went scrambling back down deep into the rabbit hole they'd been hiding in before. I shifted instinctively into practical-thinking mode. David was quiet, but there were tears streaming down his face. My mind was already racing as to what to do next. I knew Mighty Mike must once again take care of things.

"Can I please have the Saint Christopher medal from around his neck?" David asked softly.

"Dad promised it to him," I explained.

"Of course," said the taller nurse. She respectfully removed my father's fingers from the cluster of holy medals, placing his arm by his side. Together, the nurses lifted my father's head and shoulders enough to remove the medal, then they nestled it into David's outstretched and waiting palm.

"Appreciate it," David said, closing his hand over the still warm medal.

"I'm so sorry," the tall nurse said. I gave her a grateful nod, then Dave and I headed for the door to make the walk down to the waiting room and break the news to whomever from the family was still at the hospital.

The hospital was very quiet save for the sound of our sneakers and their loud squeaking on the waxed and polished floor of the corridor leading down to the waiting room. I could see through the glass on the door that only Diane, Loretta, and Susan were in there and no one else. All three turned their heads at once as I pushed open the swinging door, and they looked at us in anticipation.

"He's gone," I said matter-of-factly and with a small lump in my throat that I hid best I could, as though ashamed for them to see me less than in control. In spite of it all, weren't we all supposed to be happy now? Wasn't that the way everyone thought our whole lives that we'd feel at this moment? Not wanting him dead, but wanting him gone?

All of my sisters' eyes were already red and swollen, and they stood and hugged each other sobbing and sniffling in what looked to me to be the kind of crying you did when both sad and relieved. David began sobbing too, kind of whispering "Daddy, oh no, Daddy!" and I just hugged him hard as he cried. In between tears, we kept repeating how better off Dad was now, out of pain and no longer suffering. Yes, we all agreed, he wasn't going to get well, and like so many others who've been through such a horrible disease, it's always best for everyone when the suffering finally ends.

Dave and I disengaged from our embrace, and I reached out my hand to offer him a black onyx pinky ring my father had given to me a few days earlier to hold on to. "Here you go," I said. "He wanted you to have this too."

He took it and, looking it over, started sobbing all over again. I could only imagine he was thinking that it had come from the finger of his now-dead father. It was too much to think about. He calmed down after a moment and slipped the ring into his pocket with the medal.

"I don't want to lose them," he explained.

We all went back to the nurses' station to ask what we needed to do next and when we'd get the death certificate, etc., so that we could begin all the funeral arrangements, process the life insurance paperwork, and do any other things that needed to be taken care of. We were walking back down the hall when the elevators suddenly opened, and there was my mother with Judy.

"Damn parking garage is practically full," Judy said, seeming exasperated.

For years, my mother swore to everyone that she'd made it back to the hospital just in time before Dad died, and that he must have known she was coming and waited for her, although of course that wasn't true.

By our expressions, they knew at once that Dad was gone. As I started to speak, Ma launched into dramatic sobbing, crying, "My Georgie, my Georgie!" and then into immediate hysterics: What was she going to do? What was going to happen to *her*? She calmed down once I reassured her I'd take care of everything. Yes, I knew where the life insurance paperwork was; no, I wasn't sure of exactly when she'd be getting the check from them. Turned out Dad had a modest $6,000 policy that would cover about half the funeral expenses, leaving Ma with the other half. But to her, it was a fortune she needed to get as fast as she could, for otherwise, how would she live?

The next few days were a blur of darting back and forth between the funeral home, the church, relatives' homes, and various crappy take-out places. The wake was well attended by both sides of the family, as other than some of my mother's sisters, most thought they'd best be there for Gertie's sake. "Oh, she must be a mess! And those poor kids!" A few of Dad's coworkers from the shipping dock stopped in as well. I wore my formal military dress uniform and made sure I went around making small talk and thanking people for coming.

"Jeez, Mike," said one his cronies who I didn't know. "Too bad about Georgie! He was an all right son-of-a-bitch. Didn't take any shit from management, I'll tell ya!" Noticing my uniform, he added, "But you must see a lot of death and shit in the military, huh?"

What a goon this guy was. *Oh, yes,* I wanted to say to him, *I couldn't go a day without stepping over a dead body or two on the sidewalks at Hanscom AFB on my way to my desk job.*

"Not as much as you'd think," I muttered and moved on.

Dad was to be buried the next day at Fairview Cemetery in Hyde Park, since it turned out he'd purchased two plots—one for him and one for Ma—some years back without telling anyone. I found the paperwork in the cheap strongbox where he kept all of his private papers. As the immediate family, we were placed in a limousine by the funeral parlor personnel and led the procession right behind the hearse, first to Sacred Heart Church in Roslindale for the funeral mass and then over to Fairview.

As we planned the service, the priest asked if anyone from the family would like to say a few words about my father, but there were no takers. Father Patrick was a bit taken aback and asked me why it was no one wished to speak. All I could tell him was that we'd appreciate it if he wouldn't mind saying some things that he thought appropriate, as everyone was too upset to speak publicly. When he asked why at least I didn't wish to speak, I murmured something about having to stand by to support my mother, who I knew would need me to be there next to her. I'm not sure why no one from Dad's side wanted to share any stories or offer words of some sort, but for whatever reason, it was unanimous.

The funeral mass was somber as Father Patrick went through the prayers and rituals. There were pockets of soft sobbing, mostly on Dad's side of the aisle. My brothers and sisters wept off and on to themselves as well. The only exceptions were my mother and grandmother, who each kept repeating "my Georgie, my Georgie" and sobbing aloud, while Dad's sister, Aunt Jeanie, held Nana around the waist and Diane did the same with Ma. I just stood expressionless on Ma's other side and kept my gaze focused on the large golden crucifix at the back of the altar and the suffering face of Jesus.

As the limousine pulled away from the curb and we headed to the cemetery, my mother turned to me, her eyes red and swollen and said, "It's okay to cry, honey." She then began another jag of her own. This started some of my siblings going again too, and the limo was full of sniffling.

"I'm okay, Ma," I said, looking out the window at the dreary sky as we drove through the tree-lined parkway and past the Bajko skating rink leading to the cemetery. And strangely enough, for that moment, I really was.

CHAPTER 12

"It's okay, Ma," I said again as she dabbed her eyes with a balled-up Kleenex. "Just think about all the good memories, okay?" At first I wasn't sure if her tears were genuine, but they appeared to be, as I guess her mind had really gone back for a hard look, maybe for the first time in a long time, at that hospital room at the Deaconess as Dad lay dying next to all the flowers and get-well cards.

"I know, I will," she said. "But seeing that flag again made me miss your father so much!"

I actually believed she was speaking the truth for the first time since I could remember. Looking at the clock, I knew I needed to wrap things up. I spoke to Ma using my calmest voice, as her psychiatrist had suggested I do whenever she behaved this way. The worst thing you could do would be to overreact, as it would only encourage her to turn her sadness into anger and renewed bitterness against all those who she'd accused of "abandoning" her.

"Well, I'll be sure to take good care of it for you, okay?" I said, trying to reassure her.

"I know you will, honey, I know," she said, her sniffling now subsided.

Her ability to summon tears on demand, without effort, matched her fainting skills, but I could see this mini crying jag was coming from real emotion, and I felt a small pang of hurt for her in the pit of my stomach. So many years were lost and wasted now, so I could only imagine a tiny bundle of true and painful feelings had dug themselves in stubbornly somewhere way down in her heart, and they asserted themselves unexpectedly from time to time, surprising even her, I supposed. It actually made me feel better to think that maybe she was at least starting to react in emotionally appropriate ways from time to time in response to things from her past.

I glanced again at the wooden anniversary clock with the big plastic face. Jody and I had given it to her and Henry as a wedding gift on their first anniversary to double-check the time. The engraved plate was too tarnished to make out the letters anymore, but the hands said it was ten minutes to one.

"I'm sorry, honey," she said, now composed. "I'm just lonely, that's all. I just fucking sit here 24-7."

Between her housekeeper and all the others who came in and out all the time, that was hardly true. Again, I knew she was really referring to never seeing any of my brothers and sisters, who weren't coming back. This was just a part of her endless cycle of frustration and bitterness that punctuated our conversations during my visits or telephone calls. She could never make any one of them feel guilty enough to be manipulated to coming by again, and my trying to convince them on the side to make their own peace with her made no difference.

"I'm sorry things turned out the way they have, Ma, but it is what it is, right? We've talked about this over and over, and I wish I could change some things, but I can't. All of us, including you, have to live with our decisions, so here we are. I can't make people feel how they don't feel, and that includes you too." Then, as I had countless times over the years, I said, "This ain't *The Waltons*," although the reference was likely lost on her.

Every visit now was scripted exactly the same as the last, and I realized more and more each time I came down that something really would have to be done soon to move her someplace where she would have the professional care she needed and where there would be more control over her obsessive demands for attention, smoking, and finger-pricking. For now, I'd hang in there with her living at home as long as possible, but assisted living would have to become a reality sooner than later, and that would, sadly, be the last stop on her crazy train.

Seeing her truly alone so much these days in terms of family visits and gatherings, it saddened me to think that over the years since my father died, while most of my aunts and uncles had remained surrounded by their children and grandchildren on the big holidays like Thanksgiving and Christmas—celebrating, sharing old recipes, and repeating special family traditions like singing songs or making recipes or whatever it was that had been passed on—she had never had and never would have anything like that. Sadder still, she didn't seem to care, and of course, we didn't really have things like those to give her anyway.

Instead, on those days, she'd sit in that recliner in the dark and quiet living room, watching game shows or maybe, in quiet, puffing cigarette after cigarette and listening to all of her clocks ticking out of sync. Oh, she'd get the obligatory five-minute call from Diane, me, and probably Susan wishing her a happy holiday, and one of us might even stop by with a plate of turkey and the fixings, and maybe some flowers or a plant or a new housecoat, but that was really all there was for her on any given holiday. I suppose that genuine love might have been gone, but we continued to do these things more out of respect and the possession of at least a shred of that omnipresent sense of obligation and guilt and the reflexive need to treat the day as most others did—and to "take care of Ma."

For Ma, holidays were really only useful as fodder for her weak attempts to induce guilt while feeding her own bitterness. Since we were already acting somewhat out of that unjustified guilt, the vitriolic spew she threw was wasted on those of us who showed up; really, it was aimed at all the others who'd vanished from her life and wouldn't have to hear it anyway. Since we were in the line of fire, she couldn't help herself from firing away. The truth was, even if everyone showed up in force to fawn over her, it wouldn't be enough. It would never be enough. She'd sneer in bitterness and say it was the very least we could do because she's the mother.

When one of us did give her a call on a holiday or her birthday, she'd say, when asked, "I fucking haven't heard from anybody," even though we already knew amongst ourselves who'd called. This was all a part of the depressing script of her existence that she'd written so very long ago and from which she could never deviate. She did not know any other way to think.

"Ah, who gives a fuck," she said with venom, her tears and sadness long gone.

I shook my head and chuckled that she could still wonder why most of her grown children didn't call or come by to visit, or why it was she didn't really know any of her fourteen grandchildren and three great-grandchildren. Too often, in a waste of breath, I tried to explain to her concepts like dysfunction and how an abusive and hostile home environment was a real and pertinent part of our past and that it must be acknowledged. I encouraged her to admit that the stuff happened, at least some of it, that's all.

"Look, Ma, maybe you really don't remember any bad things," I said, "but we do, and some of them are still strong and ugly memories. Sure, they're long gone by, but they are part of what made us who we are, and what we think about when we think about the past, and what we think about you, and why things turn out in our lives the way they did."

I started down the laundry list of bad memories for which she seemed to have amnesia. The welts on my back from that beating back on Green Street. Many of us crying in the night from abscessed teeth back in the Mission Hill projects. The cockroaches and the empty cupboards. I literally shook my head to get rid of them.

"Look," I went on. "You have said it yourself, just like the shrink told you: 'perception is reality.' You've got yours, different as it may be to others, but so does everyone else. Look, think of it this way. I learned this in college," I explained, hoping to give this next idea some credibility with her.

I continued, "We're all born like little blank slates, in a way, right? Everything that we get exposed to teaches us and is what makes us who we all eventually become. Can you understand any of that?"

I could tell by her expression that it was useless. All she could do was put on the saddest of her sad faces, not really listening now it seemed, and gaze out the window and whisper, "Oh, look at the pretty bird" as a robin darted by. This was another of her classic avoidance techniques.

I had taken her a few years before to visit a geriatric psychologist at the Brigham and Women's Hospital in Boston, hoping the doctor might help her get over her finger-pricking obsession—and most important, perhaps, take responsibility for, and break through, at least some of her self-absorption. I hoped this might allow her to start to restore her relationships with some of her estranged children. Not that they'd ever even want to, but maybe if they saw a believable change in her, it might be possible, who knows.

During the session, the psychiatrist asked me if, among ourselves, we'd ever been able to sit down and have an open and honest discussion about past events that might have contributed to the family's deterioration. I started to explain that I had tried to lead such dialogues, but my mother would rush to deny any responsibility, disputing any notion that she might have had any hand in it. She'd then resort to employing the "look at the pretty bird" tactic, infuriating everyone. They'd given up agreeing to talk together years ago after a couple of attempts.

While I was explaining all that, the doctor, who'd been watching my mother's reaction, turned to her and said, "Mrs. Boudreau, did you hear what your son just said?"

The doctor shook her head in disbelief, laughing, when my mother responded by pointing out the window and saying, "Oh, look, I think it's starting to snow," providing a live demonstration of her diversionary reflex.

What a wasted trip that was, between the traffic getting into Boston, the crazy parking, and my mother's predictable obstinacy and deflections. I never took her back.

Turning to me now, and with a sad and perplexed sound of innocence in her voice, she repeated her mantra: "What didn't I do? You kids were always clean and polite, everybody said so. I was a *good* mother!" she insisted as the sobbing resumed, a bit exaggerated this time.

"Look, Ma," I said, knowing that I was sounding clinical and very much like an adjunct college professor. "Again, for the millionth time, you've got to try real hard to understand that some people still feel hurt and have grudges, no matter what you think happened, that are still with them after all these years. Specific things they feel that you are responsible for, or maybe you didn't protect them from—and you say you don't want to talk about it. Don't you get how weird that is? If you could maybe understand that, even a little bit, things might be different. But you know what? I doubt it. At least start talking about it, and maybe even take some blame for once in your life! Doesn't any of this matter to you?" I said, my voice now escalating despite my attempts at control.

"Blame for what? I didn't do nothin'!" she snapped, sounding defiant.

"Ma, you're not *listening* to me!" I said, frustrated, my voice rising.

Even when I spoke in the most simple of terms, she could not comprehend any of this. She could not see the obvious things looming and staring her square in the face that, unless she saw them, blocked any possibility for even a sniff at her getting any kind of reconciliation with any other of her children. It occurred to me that what she couldn't seem to see was that one of the most harmful things from our childhood was something that both she and Dad *didn't* do. Something they *didn't* do every day to every one of us, I'm sure without realizing it, and Ma still continued to *not* do. When I first figured out what it was, I was surprised to discover that it hurt more than any beating or a toothache ever could.

Among the many horrible things that could happen to kids growing up, including us, is looking back on your childhood and realizing that, the whole time, your parents never showed you or told you, even once, that your feelings about anything that was happening to you, or to your life, mattered to them—that *you* mattered to them.

If she could only see that what we really needed was to know that they'd, at the very least, seen how hard it was for us to change houses and schools at such a relentless pace, and deal with the constant embarrassment of wearing ill-fitting hand-me-downs, and place a hand over our mouths when we laughed or smiled to hide our black and broken teeth, and so much more. We needed to know they were sorry for having done that to us and that they knew how difficult it must have been. Most of all, we needed to know that they were sorry for how awful we must have *felt*. Was she sorry that over the years we had to discover from others that the most important thing anyone can and should do is to care for another, to show the gentle kind human spirit that binds us all, and makes us whole, because our parents didn't show us the way?

But how could they be sorry, when they were oblivious that their kids were spending their childhoods stumbling along behind them, trying to stay on their feet, trudging on over the years in their wake of psychological turbulence? If they were ever aware that we were staggering behind, they'd have had to care. Maybe if they had only turned around to take a look, give a glance, they might have. But they didn't do either. Ah, forget it now, really. It was all too far beyond repair.

As awful as it might sound for us kids to think this way about our parents, the reality we always imagined they had about us was that we arrived through random pregnancy and were placed on this earth as parasitical baggage to be hidden from the landlord so they could get that two-bedroom apartment that was limited to smaller families. Or maybe our larger purpose was as George's justification for maximum fraudulent welfare checks or those account options when changing the name on a utility bill. This was how we felt. We definitely didn't see ourselves as outcomes of wedded bliss and the union of souls, more as bit actors in their two-star play.

All of these thoughts and more had been welling up in me as they tended to, visit after visit. Although I could usually will myself to not let them get to me as much as they had this time, I felt myself losing the fight against the impulse to scream all of these thoughts at her, right then in that moment. I knew it was ridiculous, but the urge to lunge at her verbally was gaining momentum and actually scaring me a little. I imagined grabbing her by her hairy chin and making her look straight at me and *listen* as I barraged her with the lifetime of charges and questions that were now racing through my agitated mind.

My pulse was quickening as I saw myself about to yell questions at her like, "Don't you get, *at all*, just how you and Georgie were so uncaring and blind to how we were getting our minds and bodies flogged for decades as we tried, in desperation, to digest all of the moving, the beatings, the changing of schools, the cockroaches, the constant loss of friends, the ridicule, the growling tummies, the rotten teeth, the freezing rooms, the old clothes? How every cruel thing you did and decision you made in isolation affected every one of us so much and in so many ways while we were at your unforgiving mercy?"

For me in particular, the worst of all that happened to us was definitely the blur of moves from one place to the next. I once stumbled upon a passage in Jack Kerouac's book *The Town and the City* that told the story of a fictional family he'd created, the Martins. They moved frequently throughout a city that resembled Kerouac's own hometown of Lowell, Massachusetts. In referring to what it was like for the Martin children to be shifted from place to place, Jack described it as "a catastrophe of their hearts. What dreams children have of walls and doors and ceilings that they always knew, what terror they have on waking up at night in strange new rooms, disarrayed and unarranged, all frightful and unknown."

"Don't you care about how any of us felt about having no sense of *place?*" I imagined myself demanding. "Did you even give any thought or feel any regret at all about anything that happened to us every single time we got dragged to a new house?" That was the million-dollar question, wasn't it?

Though I still hadn't moved, I saw myself looming over her now as she cowered and I continued my shouting: "Do you know just how much you fed my sisters' fears that any night might be the night Georgie decided to make good on his threats to show them how a real man satisfies a woman as he had threatened he would when we heard those muffled voices from your bedroom? Do you know how petrified of that my sisters were? They were just young girls. Can you imagine the horror of them having to endure listening to their own mother telling them all this only to do nothing to shield them or reassure them, nothing to make them feel safe?"

Continuing my interrogation, I'd demand to know if she remembered the time when my father did make a move on my oldest sister while Ma was in the hospital having Susan, and upon her return home, her telling—almost accusing—Diane with "I tried to warn you girls"?

"Tell me then," I saw myself yelling, "why was it that with Susan, your last-born child, you and Dad broke the tradition of sending all of us to stay with family and had just Diane staying home, left alone with Dad? Speaking of Susan, do you perchance recollect the countless times after Dad died that you told her you never really wanted her and the only reason you became pregnant with her in the first place was because he raped you?"

Since she, of course, would say she didn't see or recall any of those disturbing things, I supposed she also would deny all knowledge if I asked her, "Did you know that Judy kept a butcher knife under her mattress for years until Loretta tattled on her? Or did you know that after all? And if by chance you did, maybe you can also remember that Dad took the knife away and beat Judy black and blue for that one? Okay, suppose you do remember that, then perhaps you also knew that Judy still took no chances and started bringing a glass upstairs to bed each night, telling me she figured she could smack it against the side of the nightstand table and cut his damn throat?"

Like Karen, Judy would never likely be his target, as he knew that she was not easy prey and would fight back. But she couldn't have known that for sure.

I was losing it now. My thoughts were racing almost out of control, and my heart was pounding. I felt the urge to move, to shout. Why not just give it to her now? What would it matter? She had it coming to her, and who better than me to let her have it? There was so much more I wanted and needed to get out that I could barely keep up with my own thoughts—not only for myself but for every one of my brothers and sisters. I felt the need to burst and let out all of this pent-up emotion, just the way I did that night with my father in the kitchen on Bradeen Street those many years ago. This putrid acid I felt bubbling up to my throat needed to go somewhere, and what better way to purge it than to spew it all over her living room?

But I couldn't do it.

Maybe it was because above all of my racing thoughts, I heard one of them telling me, as it whispered persistently over the din of all the others, to just *calm down and listen.* I finally did, and then I heard something profound and important, maybe even obvious. It had been niggling in the background at me for years, especially when I let her get me worked up, and although I could never make it out, now here it was.

None of what she did or didn't do, to any one of us, from watching the beatings to making us her allies against my father, came from even the slightest measure of actual hatred toward us in her heart. She may have hated the way things were for her growing up or turned out in her marriage, or the way her children were now scattered from her life, who knows—but she didn't act the way she did all those years as we were growing up, I believed, out of malice.

Maybe it was that she simply didn't experience complete maternal love herself—what it meant and was *supposed* to be—and without knowledge of that, the purest of all loves, she did not know how to do what was needed and expected of her when she became a mother herself. Maybe the denial of that almost inexpressibly strong love that can exist between a mother and her children was among the many things that had impacted her own childhood and made her feel abandoned and uncared for. I could only guess. Once she got married, maybe that's when she began looking to my father, and subsequently her children, to fill the void of "taking care of her"—and, as it would turn out, do so at the expense of her taking care of us.

As all this went through my mind, that calm voice was telling me to hang on, that I'd be out of there in just a few minutes and to just take a breath and really look at her and see her for who she was now: a pitiable lost old lady whose life had taken whatever turns it had in bringing her to this moment—and she was still my mother. Now I only saw a small, stooped, and sad stranger who seemed genuinely lost and confused. All I could do was wonder where the mother who woke me up for hot chocolate and Hershey bars so many Christmases ago had gone.

No, the individual hurts or collateral damage that resulted from growing up with the woman who now sat across from me, whatever that might mean to any of us, was done. Our relationship with who had been, at least at one time, a semblance of our mother was simply broken down or gone. The psychologist in me was now in control of my emotions, and I knew that nothing—not any screaming or crying or pleading by anyone— could ever do anything to change one single bad memory or one stabbing pain from an abscessed tooth, and it certainly couldn't change anything about her now or do her any good.

The emotional bridge had been burned, and I knew there was nothing she could really ever do to gain forgiveness for herself, even if she wanted it, because as far as I could tell, she'd lost any ability to feel guilt or remorse about anything. In the end, there just wasn't enough love left, on either side, to do the job. Forgiveness was now up to each one of us to give on our own terms, even without any expression of regret or sorrow from her. It was all so very sad and pathetic, and my heart filled with pity for her and for all of us—and sadness for the loss of so much unexpressed love and what might have been shared between so many.

The truth was that now, we'd each have to face a choice between being a scarred but accepting survivor of a sort—embracing life focused on the best from the future and the freedom that dumping the ugly parts of the past could bring—or remaining tethered to a useless seething anger like a self-determined and perpetual psychological victim, bitter and half-living inside, wallowing in pity about a history that could never be changed and was clearly better left behind.

There were no other options. It always comes back to that good old locus of control. I kept a framed quote from the inspirational writer Catherine Ponder in my office: "When you hold resentment toward another, you are bound to that person or condition by an emotional link that is stronger than steel. Forgiveness is the only way to dissolve that link and get free." It seemed to me it was the unwillingness to forgive that continued to course through my family and kept forgiveness from unleashing its healing power and unlocking the steel chains of bitterness.

There it was. Dad was long dead. Ma was old, called crazy by most, and left now to answer to her children for everything from the past and present—something she could never do. There would be no earthly confessions or regrets from either of them, no matter how desperately they might be wished for. With no confession, of course, there could never be forgiveness given or penance performed. There could be no cleansing of the soul, no growing through grace, but only hopeful new beginnings for those willing to accept what was and leave behind an imperfect past with as much dignity and mercy as possible.

We could only trust in a higher power's wisdom—the kind of wisdom that tells you to do such things as count your blessings and make inexplicable biweekly visits to your frustrating old mother, because in spite of anything, it is the right thing to do, and the kind of wisdom that prevents you from wasting even one day looking back at a dark hole that can never be filled but rather keeps all eyes looking forward toward the light. It's okay to be pissed off in the moment or at a memory. How could that be helped? Looking forward was all that was left.

I thought of a scene from the movie *Forrest Gump* when he and his girlfriend Jenny were taking a stroll in the Alabama countryside. They stumbled across the decrepit and abandoned house in which she'd been terribly abused as a little girl growing up. Jenny became hysterical at the flood of memories that the place held for her and began to pick up every rock in sight, hurling them angrily and uselessly at the rotting building until she was too exhausted to go on. Forrest just stood there silent, watching with sadness, and when she was done he turned to her and said, "Sometimes, I guess there just aren't enough rocks."

I supposed he was telling her that sometimes the hurt is so big that ultimately, you will have to let go of it, even before you reach the point where you think you are ready or willing to, because if you don't, you may never get to that place in your heart that allows you to stop throwing rocks at the ones who hurt you. Getting to that place is really what it takes to let you move forward and understand that it is not just the letting go itself, not just the forgetting, but the *forgiving* that will release and strengthen you so that you can grow and prosper. I'd say Forrest knew a thing or two about wisdom.

A part of the Bible I heard so long ago in the beautiful Mission Church when the priest read from the book of the apostle Mark had been seared in my memory: "When you stand to pray, forgive anyone against whom you have a grievance, so that your heavenly Father may in turn forgive your transgressions." All of us need to let go and stay in that place in our hearts that tells us to forgive no matter what or who may have offended or hurt us, especially when any dark road or memory of those offenses might lead us back to anger.

For me, even as I struggled from time to time with my own groundswells of emotion, and it might not seem like it to me all the time, inside I knew that I really had moved on and let go of any kind of chronic hate or resentment—for either of my parents. I mean, after all, I'd once joked to one of my sisters that if Ma had decided to put ketchup on her Kotex the day I was conceived, I might not even be here, so I guess I owed her one.

I'd accepted things as they were as far as what growing up had been, but what drove me most crazy now and during these visits was how she and most of the rest of my family continued to live their lives in a vicious swirling whirlpool of unresolved conflict, full of accusations and denials about the past. I'd all too often almost allow myself to be sucked into its vortex, but somehow I always managed to crawl my way out, time and time again.

I didn't get drawn into family drama because I needed any type of inner healing or apologies. It was just that no matter how much I had let go of any residual crap like theirs, there was a part of me that would react with emotion to what was going on around me, because like it or not, it came with being part of a family. In spite of how sideways this one may have been, it was the one I had, and I just couldn't help but care—even if there wasn't anything Mighty Mike could do about the most troubling things.

I didn't want or need a formal apology or anything more from my mother other than for her to try to make any kind of effort to treat others better and to at least acknowledge and care about the facts of the past as best she could, which wasn't saying much. I'd long forgiven her without needing to hear her confession. I did have to wonder, though, if she too would give in and turn to God for forgiveness in her final hours, if given the chance, for any kind of absolution and perhaps rejoin with Dad in purgatory, where I was pretty sure (maybe more like hopeful) he was still hanging out after all these years if he'd even gotten that far. I could just imagine my father's welcome with his usual style: "Holy shit, can you believe we *both* got here?"

As far as wanting anything from any of my siblings, I hoped for nothing other than for them to somehow figure out for themselves how to get past bitter feelings about not having mattered or whatever else was crawling around in their heads or upsetting their inner child. As wounded as I knew some of them were, I suppose each in his or her way had a right to be. I wanted them to abandon the notion that Ma would or even could have some sudden epiphany and make it all right. I hoped they would discover as I had over the years that through all the blessings and countless other wonderful people that came into my life, I had *mattered* all along, and my siblings did too. I wanted them to do these things for their own hearts and minds and inner peace.

Feeling clammy now, I shut my eyes for a second to steady my breathing and slow my heaving chest, reminding myself of all of that and remembering my last words to my father. I had to admit that this was about the closest I'd come to lighting her up. *Better not let Jody leave me alone with her anymore*, I chuckled to myself, thinking of Norman Bates and Loretta's alter, Bob.

"I do think about everything you say. I listen to you!" Ma was now protesting, not having noticed anything unusual about me as I wiped sweat from my brow with my sleeve. "I just don't remember any of that bad stuff everybody keeps saying happened!"

"Well, Ma, again, I'm sorry, but it is what it is." I felt my skin cooling off a little as my pulse slowed and the blood drained from my face. The spell broken, I got up from the arm of the couch. It was time to go.

Recognizing the signs of my departure, Ma said, "Are you taking me to the doctor's next week? I need my labs drawn, and Diane says she can't take me this time."

"I'll talk with Susan, and I'm sure she'll take you. I gotta work. I'll text her and then let you know later tonight, okay?" I replied.

"You won't forget to call me?" she said, sounding a little extra desperate and needy now, almost childlike.

"No, I promise, I'll call later once I find out." And I would too, knowing she'd obsess over it until I did and call my sisters nonstop until she got the answer, because she was "nervous."

"Oh," she said, as if she'd forgotten something. She weakly stood up from her recliner and grabbed for the handles of her walker. "I wanted to show you how I arranged some of my dolls on my dresser in the bedroom." She started to shuffle the walker toward the hallway.

"No, Ma," I said, cutting her off. "I have to go. I'll see it next time, okay?"

This was similar to her "look at the bird" maneuver to try to get me to prolong my visit, and I knew that if I let her, she would go from one distraction to another to delay my departure.

She plunked back down in the recliner, looking disappointed. It was just about one o'clock.

"Okay, maybe next time," she said, her voice feeble.

"Ma, I'm sorry, but I've got errands to run, and we've got company coming for dinner, so we gotta go shopping and stuff. I'll call you later and see you in two weeks, okay?"

"Oh, okay, thank you for coming," she said meekly, sounding almost formal, as if she were saying goodbye to a slight acquaintance who had stopped by for a bit to have a cup of tea. I ignored that and focused on a guilt-free exit as her doctor suggested, and as I knew I must. It was getting easier all the time. I bent down and kissed her forehead.

"Take it easy, okay?" I sighed.

"Okay," she said, sniffling.

"Hey, and don't forget, the Red Sox are on tonight at seven!" I said to change the mood.

"Oh, good! What time and what channel?" she said, brightening a little.

"Seven o'clock on channel 262," I said, trying to leave her on an upbeat note. "I'll write it down for you, okay?" I reached for the pad of paper on the end table next to her overflowing ashtray. "There, you're all set."

"You won't forget to call me later?"

"No, I won't forget, Ma. Gotta go now. Okay?

As I walked down the short flight of stairs and was about to touch the handle on the screen door, she called out, "I love you. And Jody too," she added through new tears I knew weren't because I was leaving but more for herself—one last shot at applying guilt.

"I love you too," I said, pausing at the door. Looking back for a moment over my shoulder, I could see the top of her head, and her fragile right arm hanging limp, draped over the arm of the chair. In that moment, I found myself hoping, not for the first time, that she'd had, at least once, known real love in her life and given it in kind. I felt sad for all the true loneliness she now had, and all that I knew she would come to know as she lived out the rituals that had become her life.

I let the screen door slam and rattle behind me and motioned to Jody that we were leaving as I waved to the neighbor. Jody exchanged final pleasantries, and we converged on the car.

"I'll drive," I said, clicking the red button on the fob key to unlock the doors.

I wanted to tell Jody just how close I'd come to having "the meltdown" this visit, but I didn't want to rehash the whole thing. Maybe I would later, after I'd given myself a good talking to and a strong drink.

We were pretty quiet until we jumped onto Route 128N heading to Route 3. I could tell we were both starting to feel that familiar sense of relief and liberation you get after leaving a painful visit to the dentist or quitting a crappy job and not caring, at least for the moment, about what happens next. Knowing we were putting Sanford Street in our rearview mirror for at least two full weeks made the next visit seem a psychological lifetime away.

"You know ..." Jody started to say as I passed the Needham exit.

"I *know*, I know, we have to start thinking about a home for her. I *get* it!" I said, finishing her sentence with exasperation.

"I'm just *kidding*," Jody said, laughing. "I'm pushing your buttons."

"Ha, ha," I said. "You got me." I tried to sound annoyed, but I couldn't help smiling back at her.

I relaxed my grip on the wheel as the tension slipped away with each mile as we headed north and began chatting with grateful enthusiasm about our trip to the lake in New Hampshire with friends that was coming up the following free weekend. This visit under our belts and now nearly forgotten, we set our sights on our waiting bar stools and the reward of a much-needed dirty martini.

I could picture Ma back on Sanford Street, sitting dry-eyed in her blue recliner with the television off and her head back as she rocked gently in time to the loudest of the ticking clocks, tapping her slipper and humming an old Tammy Wynette song, cigarette perched gingerly in her hand. I could see her inhaling deeply from her Benson and Hedges 100 menthol cigarette and then, with a heavy sigh, exhaling the smoke through her nostrils and gazing with a blank expression as she watched it drift lazily into the shadows in the far corner of the living room.

EPILOGUE

None of us could remember the last time Mom had been this dressed up. Her appearance was jarring after seeing her pretty much wigless and unkempt for so many years, just sitting as she did in the dark living room in that old blue recliner wearing her flannel pajamas, tattered robe, and slippers. Everyone remarked how youthful and beautiful she looked now in the pretty lavender dress with the soft white sweater draped over her shoulders, her coiffed wig perfectly in place, and her serene face softened by many years thanks to the amazing work of a gifted makeup artist. All of her favorite jewelry was strung around her neck, and her prized rings adorned her fingers, which were placed, intertwined, in final repose on her abdomen.

David and I made a point of going into the room first to see her and to make sure we were satisfied that she'd been properly cared for and was as presentable as we knew she'd have wanted to be. And she was. We knelt at the portable altar that had been placed in front of her casket, and silently, and almost in unison, made the sign of the cross and bowed our heads, each of us saying a quick but private prayer.

David reached out, twisted, and straightened one of the rings on her left hand to align it with the others. The air in the room was thick with the scent of the flowers that surrounded the casket and ran the length of the wall on either side. All were adorned with silk sashes, and each had a small note card from the sympathetic donor attached. Soft hymnal music was playing in the background. I glanced at the closed half of the casket where we'd had her name and dates of birth and death engraved, along with a pair of crossed hockey sticks just beneath. Knowing how much Ma loved to watch her Bruins, it was Susan's idea when we were making the arrangements.

Susan had also arranged for some of Ma's favorite things to be placed around her. There was the dusty airman doll I sent her from somewhere long ago that was dressed in a small air force uniform with my rank insignia pinned to its shoulders, and her favorite shawl was folded over her legs and lap. For some reason, there was also a can of Campbell's cream of chicken soup and a box of Mueller's elbow macaroni in there as well.

"What's with the soup and pasta?" I asked Dave.

"Ah," Susan said, "that's all Ma would eat for dinner anymore, so she wanted to put it in there. I didn't think you'd care."

"No, of course not," I said. "Weird. But make sure they put Buffalo wings in with me, okay?"

"Sure," Dave said, mustering a small chuckle.

It was Susan who came home on that frigid early evening in late January to a dark house and living room, quiet except for the low volume coming from the television that flickered soft light on the ceiling and walls. Climbing the short flight of stairs from the front door of the split-level ranch, she turned at the top to see a 1970s episode of *Let's Make a Deal* on the Game Show Network—with some excited woman dressed like a banana jumping up and down in excitement—and at what she thought was Ma slumped over and sleeping in her chair. Susan had moved in downstairs with her husband while she was waiting on her new apartment and was a great help to Ma and to all of us by being there.

As she got closer to the chair, she knew at once that something wasn't right. Susan shook Ma's arm in an attempt to wake her, but she was gone. I'll never forget Susan's frantic phone call. I tried to get her to calm down and talk her through what to do next, all the while wishing it was anyone but Susan who had found Ma in that blue recliner, as she had too many times heard my mother, in her most bitter moments, threaten that that's exactly how it would happen, and how everyone would be happy then, wouldn't they?

"She looks good, she looks good," David said, as though trying to say something positive.

"Yes, she does," I said. "First time I've seen her smile in years," I joked weakly.

"I know, right?" Dave said. "These guys do a great job here, and I knew they'd take good care of her."

Dave had worked for the funeral home on and off over the years since he was a teenager—painting, wall-papering, gardening, and the like. He knew all of the family going back a couple of generations, just as he did about most of the families in business in and around Cleary Square. He'd built solid relationships with them all, and they were quick to offer any support to him and our family that they could out of genuine affection for him.

"Well, guess it's time to let the drama begin," I said, hearing Loretta sobbing outside in the lobby—first in line, I was sure, behind the heavy double doors.

"Yup, let's do this," David said with a sigh as we got up in unison. I absentmindedly brushed my fingers over the hockey sticks on the bronze casket, thinking how such beautiful etching would soon be out of sight from the world forever.

I pushed the doors outward toward the lobby and secured them by clicking the doorstops into place with my foot. The viewing was scheduled for five to eight in the evening, and it was about quarter past five. All of my siblings, save Eddie, were milling about the lobby, looking at old photographs of Ma that had been mounted to poster boards and placed on tripods scattered by either side of the entrance door. Most were in black and white, showing my mother either pregnant or smoking a cigarette or both.

Loretta and Susan were having a tough time dealing with their emotions, but everyone else was subdued and composed—trying, I supposed, to figure out how to feel now that Ma was suddenly gone, along with her constant demands for attention and the endless vitriol she expressed against each one of us in whichever particular way I'm sure she felt would be most effective. I could sense that all the rest of us, except maybe for Judy, were trying to be careful to find the appropriate balance between expressing genuine grief while perhaps fighting guilty feelings for a sense of relief. Since she'd declared herself emotionally divorced from my mother many years before, Judy seemed more like a family friend, almost indifferent to Ma's having died but rather focused on her real concern for the rest of us.

Other than my mother's youngest brother, Paul, none of her remaining siblings attended the wake or funeral. I stood in the receiving line with Judy, David, Karen, and Diane, and I watched him as he sat facing the front of the casket in the otherwise empty row of chairs, staring at Ma, deep in his own thoughts. I remembered a day long ago when we lived on the house on Hyde Park Avenue where I got that new red bike, when Uncle Paul had come home from the air force on leave in his perfect blue uniform—the very one I'd wear so many years later.

Aunt Esther had hoped to come down from New Hampshire for the funeral, but Boston was being slammed yet again with a major winter storm, making travel impossible for her. Neither of Ma's two other living siblings—my Aunt Betty and Ma's youngest half-sister, Evelyn—even acknowledged her death.

As we stood in that receiving line, not many came through to offer condolences other than a few kind cousins from the O'Brien and Bovaird families, one of my mother's day nurses, and the funeral home staff. As Ma was getting older and more and more solitary, Jody and I sometimes mused that it wouldn't be surprising if when she died her services would be poorly attended. Ma had kept no lifelong friends or relationships and had so alienated herself over the years from so many, including her own family, that her passing, acknowledged by so few, appeared unnoticed by the world.

I kept glancing over at her quiet, separate presence and found myself wishing the people who were there would move closer to the casket to make me feel that somehow she wasn't so alone. But she was. I thought back to when my mother's sister, Aunt Louise O'Brien, had left her family and the world way too soon, and the amazing love that surrounded her at her wake as I watched all of the O'Brien children form a semicircle in front of her casket and sing "When Irish Eyes Are Smiling" for her, just as they had so often sung together with her as they grew up, I'm sure.

But there was no choir to be heard here—just the almost inaudible funereal music playing in the background. No, there was just the quiet shuffle of people moving around the room, whispering in small clusters as though at a private cocktail party, chatting amongst themselves, their hostess all but ignored. I listened as one by one, people offered final condolences to some of my siblings and then excused themselves after completing whatever they considered to be the obligatory time to call as the funeral home staff opened the door, releasing them to the darkness and the howling and bitter winter wind.

Although the viewing was to be from five to eight o'clock, by six thirty everyone had come and gone, leaving just me and those of my siblings who wished to linger behind to spend time alone with Ma in private thought. Only Dave and I chose to do so before meeting with the funeral director to go over the final plans for Ma's burial at Fairview Cemetery in the morning. There would be no funeral mass, no church celebration—just a deacon secured by the funeral home for a fee who would stop by in the morning to say a few words before the immediate family followed the hearse over to Fairview Cemetery, where Dad would be waiting.

I woke to a brilliant, clear, and bitter day that saw the wind still whipping without mercy over the snowbanks that covered the city's sidewalks, making it impossible to turn any corner without first inching out to see. We all met at eight o'clock in morning at the funeral home and took up just two rows of folding chairs lined up in front of the casket. Everyone was quiet and staring straight ahead when the deacon, who'd been waiting for the last person to take a seat, began reading from the scriptures with the appropriate amount of reverence for the occasion. When he finished, he asked if anyone would like to say a few words, but just as it was at my father's funeral mass so many years before, no one moved.

The dozen or so cars were already lined up against the snowbank in front of the funeral home, my pickup truck in place to lead the convoy. As we waited for the hearse to pull out to begin the procession, Jody and I sat in the cab of the truck, shivering as the heat worked its way up. We were quiet, much the way we were on those rides in to Readville toting groceries and cigarettes on all of those Saturday mornings. Looking in my rearview mirror, I could see the other cars warming up as well, steam billowing from their exhaust pipes against the frigid air.

The hearse finally pulled into view to my right coming down the long driveway from the funeral home. One of the staff signaled to me to follow, so I popped on the emergency flashers, as did those behind me, and we began the short two mile or so ride to the cemetery. As we pulled up the drive toward my father's gravesite, I realized I hadn't been there in at least fifteen years and wondered why. David made frequent trips to check out the condition of the stone, clear off any leaves that may have gathered, and maybe place some fresh flowers.

By the time I pulled up, the hearse had already arrived and centered my mother's casket over the freshly unearthed grave. I was surprised the city of Boston would be able to open gravesites in such harsh weather and with the ground frozen. The gravesite was on a high steep slope of land, now slippery with patches of ice and snow. The headstone faced the Blue Hills in Canton, and the ski trail there could clearly be seen off in the distance. The deacon was about halfway down to the casket and motioned for us to join him there at that safe distance on a large dry spot. All was quiet except for the sound of the snow crunching under feet and the screech of a couple of crows scolding us in the nearby trees.

I shuffled gingerly, walking almost sideways next to David. He turned with a wry smile and said, "Well, at least she'll be back on top where she liked it best." I had to smirk a little because like me, he couldn't resist humor at the strangest times.

We all stood in the cold, faces tightening against the lashing wind, as the deacon recited some final scripture, wishing my mother the speediest trip to heaven to join Dad and, most important, our heavenly father.

"For as much as it has pleased Almighty God to take out of this world the soul of Gertrude, we therefore commit her body to the ground, earth to earth, ashes to ashes, dust to dust, looking for that blessed hope when the Lord Himself shall descend from heaven with a shout, with the voice of the archangel, and with the trumpet of God, and the dead in Christ shall rise first. Then we which are alive and remain shall be caught up together with them in the clouds to meet the Lord in the air, and so shall we ever be with the Lord, wherefore comfort ye one another with these words."

With that, we each made the sign of the cross before making the careful climb back up the slope to the still warm vehicles. As I walked, I found myself musing back to my thoughts of the night about my cousins, the O'Briens, and how they celebrated my aunt Louise in song through their tears and sadness. I thought how wonderful it would be if everyone's life was celebrated like that somehow, especially as we mourn their death. How great it would be if some expression of a deep and communal grief grounded in the profound sense of loss that comes from the strength of the love felt for the one now lost would cause God to smile at the sight and take our loved one by the hand in a gesture that says, "You've done well. Welcome."

In that moment, I found myself wanting that for Ma. But as she lay there at the wake last night all but ignored, all I could sense was that the room was void of even the smallest vibration of communal loss. I imagined that it would take all the private thoughts and prayers for her salvation, by those so inclined, to somehow collide and collect themselves together as one over time and do as best they could to boost her chances of gaining God's grace and maybe her final peace. I cranked the truck's engine. Glancing back in the mirror, I could see the cemetery staff already working to lower Ma's casket into the open grave to join Dad. While looking at that final image of my mother leaving this world, I had already begun to give her mine.

As we pulled away, Jody and I turned to each other, each about to speak. As if she was reading my mind, Jody said, "Looks like we've taken our last ride in to Readville."

No more Saturday or Sunday mornings at the base commissary filling a grocery cart with orange juice and cream of chicken soup. No more keeping close watch on her ticking living room clock eager to get away from our visits. No more stopping by the bar to see Scott on the way home for the medicating martinis. All of those countless, complaint-filled trips to Sanford Street almost every other weekend and the meager fifteen-minute visits now seemed so trivial a sacrifice compared to the countless other blessings in my life—a life that Ma had given to me.

Jody and I slipped without words into our own thoughts, almost oblivious to the sound of the truck keys swaying and clacking against the steering column as I maneuvered the truck through the bumpy, narrow, and winding cemetery roads. We passed the rows of polished headstones, weathered crosses, and an army of life-sized angels and then headed out through the enormous black wrought iron gate.

Small pangs of sorrow, or something else, now worked their way from my heart up into my throat, making me swallow hard as my eyes, now blinking back an unexpected wetness, took one long last look in the rearview mirror. I stared at the reflection of the place where my parents would now be together once more, waiting in helpless silence for the prayers and forgiveness of their children, and only God knows who else, that I knew their souls so desperately needed to somehow begin.

HARD TO SAY WHY ON MISSION HILL
PART II

The big and blinding snowflakes melted as fast as they fell, wet on the warm windshield,
My car winding down the Fenway, leaving Mission Hill to the final dimming of the day.
Sigh followed sigh, as memories shifted to a sunny Saturday on a scruffy baseball field,
The one next to the red brick rectory where we played all day starting weekends in May.

I was at the plate, my head dwarfed by my bat, a prized oversized Mickey Mantle
Bought at Woolworth's with money made from helping a friend deliver the Sunday Globe.
I saw the smirks and heard the stifled snickers as I waggled the bat, struggling to wield its weight.
The pitch came almost like a lob, and my swing and miss brought a murmur of giggles.

I lunged weakly at the next pitch, although it was a bit short, and they all saw strike two.
Giggles became laughter as I choked up on the bat, about to strike out. That's certain, they knew.
The third pitch came with a bit more zip, so I shut my eyes and swung awkwardly, inside out.
The crack of the bat startled me as the ball ripped down the foul line, and they started to shout.

Frozen for a second in disbelief, I watched as it hit the dusty first-base bag then kicked to the right,
Sending the right fielder and first baseman scrambling frantically after it as I rounded first.
The crowd yelled "Run!" then "Get down!" as I closed in, arms pumping, on second base.
"Slide!" they cried as I dove head first, in safe with a double, dirt covering my beaming face.

I started singing "Sherry Baby" along with the Four Seasons in time with the wipers' beat.
Semicircles of slush formed at the far edges of the windshield, making me lean to peek
To find the street signs that led to Route 1 North to get me at last to Route 128 and home,
And, for now, far from that field, far from those roaches, but never too far from feeling alone.

ABOUT THE AUTHOR

Michael Boudreau grew up in Boston, the third eldest of eight children. After traveling the world for twenty-eight years with the United States Air Force, he returned home to settle in Massachusetts. He holds a master of arts degree in community social psychology from the University of Massachusetts, Lowell, and serves as an adjunct professor of psychology at local undergraduate universities.